MUSEUM CATALOGUES

a foundation for
computer processing

MUSEUM CATALOGUES
a foundation for
computer processing

Brian Abell-Seddon

CLIVE BINGLEY LONDON

© Brian Abell-Seddon 1987

Published by
Clive Bingley Limited
7 Ridgmount Street
London WC1E 7AE

First published 1988

British Library Cataloguing in Publication Data

Abell-Seddon, Brian
  Museum catalogues : a foundation for computer
  processing.
  1. Museum registration methods——Data processing
  I. Title
  069.5'2'02854   AM139

  ISBN 0-85157-429-7

Printed and made in Great Britain by Redwood Burn Ltd, Trowbridge, Wiltshire

An infamous notice in an exhibition gallery announced:

'This case is not intended to illustrate anything except
our lack of space.'

(Blackwood, 1970)

Applied to catalogue records, the declaration might be:

'This catalogue is not intended to disclose anything except
our lack of organisation.'

To every curator who aims to renounce that confession,
this book is dedicated.

Contents

Foreword

It is a pleasure to write in commendation of Brian Abell-Seddon's book and the system of museum catalogue organisation he proposes. He has christened it, a little tongue-in-cheek, REFORM --- an acronym for Reference Framework for Organising Records in Museums. If this sounds daunting, intending readers should take heart from the rigorously logical way in which he analyses the problem, and his lucid exposition of the solution and its practical application. He brings to the subject the scientific discipline he acquired as a natural historian, a field where taxonomy has been wrought into a highly refined instrument for the precise codification of knowledge.

He has had many years practical experience as a museum curator working in large, multi-disciplinary museums at Cardiff and Birmingham. The breadth and diversity of the Birmingham collections and, one must add, the accumulation of disparate systems of departmental classification in relation to a centralised inventory, caused problems that would test the ingenuity of any registrar. Now that computer technology and information retrieval have become so sophisticated and capable of very wide application, the means are there for those willing to adopt and adapt them for museum use.

Dr. Abell-Seddon acknowledges the efforts of others in this field, not least the Museum Documentation Association's pioneering work in establishing a record framework which can be used on computer systems. He is careful to call his proposals "a foundation", and would welcome further debate about them. The publication of this book should certainly stimulate more discussion, but I believe it does contain a practical answer to the problem of reconciling the differing needs of specialist curatorial departments to the requirements of a centralised database. It incorporates a multi-tier system which provides flexibility within a clearly defined matrix, but avoids the anarchic chaos that still haunts the records of even some of our most presitigious institutions.

Dennis Farr
Director, Courtauld Institute Galleries, University of London.

Author's preface

This book takes as its starting-point the catalogues that already exist in most museums, galleries and heritage collections. In many cases these have remained in typescript and handwritten forms of varying content and arrangement with little attempt to rationalise the records or to improve their accessibility. In this work, the first three chapters examine a variety of object records of this type, drawn from actual museum catalogues, and these are critically reviewed. The question is "How can varied and inconsistent styles of record be reconciled?" In response, by using an analytical method it is shown how freely written text can be converted into better organised form while avoiding the complete disintegration of description into form-filling jargon. The system of cataloguing explained in this work is new in conception and it departs from some assumptions inherent in already published schemes.

There are many curators working in museums who find it difficult to regard information as a commodity that can be managed independently of the collections to which it refers. To help overcome this difficulty, issues that are fundamental to all catalogues are discussed on a wide-ranging basis and so a new perspective is provided in which all museum collections are seen to reflect a common spectrum of object-centred information. Having introduced a new conceptual framework to which both old and new records can be related, guidelines are given for various computer strategies that can be developed. The objective is to improve the supply of information through access to catalogue data and related records for effective management of collections and in response to public expectations. In the writer's opinion, public interest and support for museums depend increasingly on the availability of inform-ation about their collections as a resource for exploration. It is hoped that a fresh evaluation of this important aspect of curatorship will interest both professionals and volunteers in museums and art galleries. Equally, I hope that owners and exhibitors of heritage properties, who have inventories to maintain and recognise limitations in their existing documentation, will find this review of concepts and methods helpful.

Acknowledgments

In our working lives we are subject to an ever-present but imperceptible
flux of background radiation, in this case comprising particles of knowledge emanating from colleagues' conversations in the daily course of
professional life. Many of my colleagues have contributed unwittingly
to the broad coverage of museum concepts and to the distillation of
experience on which the book is founded and they deserve recognition.
My special thanks are due to Dr. Dennis Farr, Director of the Courtauld
Galleries, University of London, who generously agreed to read the draft
and made helpful suggestions: it is a particular pleasure to include
his Foreword. The numbered Examples are real records reproduced by kind
permission of Michael Diamond, Director of Birmingham City Museums and
Art Gallery. Only the names of living persons have been altered. The
example describing a military uniform and several brief quotations from
articles published in MDA Information are included by permission of the
Museum Documentation Association, which is gratefully acknowledged.

Chapter 1

Introduction

There are many members of the museum profession who doubt that a general pattern can be found underlying the variety of catalogues and documentary requirements of unique collections. This point of view is understandable by anyone familiar with the diversity of museums' interests and specialisms, extending from art galleries in all their forms to industrial and historical museums in which working displays and reconstructed scenarios are principal features. Despite this spectacular variety of museum manifestations, it is absurd to claim that there are not aspects of common concern to cataloguers, whatever the nature of collections: indeed the actual components of information recorded about objects are largely common ground. Admittedly, dissimiliar terms are used by curators in various specialisms to refer to comparable aspects and this gives rise to the belief that a uniform basis for recording is, if not unattainable, at least without practical merit.

An art curator is concerned with artists as creators of the works in his gallery; a technology curator is interested in the inventors and the manufacturers of industrial products, equally to be recognised as creators of the objects involved. The archaeologist is often denied knowledge of the original maker (as an individual) of artefacts in his collections but is acutely aware of the relevance of the sites where they were discovered. In this concern the archaeological curator shares a

1

common interest with the curator of natural history and geological specimens. The list of shared concerns extends virtually throughout the entire range of museological data and is merely disguised by the terms applied in the context of different subject specialisations.

This conclusion is of major significance for curators and museum directors because it means that improvements in documentary methods, catalogue standards and so on are to be found by looking for signposts outside the confines of a single subject. The structural bones of a model record can be derived from observing documentary developments in all fields of collecting, leading to the thesis of an underlying unity in the structure of museum records. This has a compelling attraction for multi-disciplinary museums in so far as the catalogues and management records of all their collections can be brought together under the umbrella of a comprehensive system with uniform standards. This is quite a different matter from the quest sometimes pursued for a binding set of conventions that will enable all museums to become parts of one global catalogue. In this regard, museums differ fundamentally from libraries: the necessity for uniformity is not compelling because objects in museum collections are not products ordered from the manufacturer nor is public access to catalogues of their collections a common facility.

The present work begins with a review of the limitations of older catalogue records, of a type which can be found in most museums, as a legacy of documentary practices from a less demanding age. While taking a critical view of the style in which information was generally recorded, we can appreciate the wealth of information they contain as constituting a valuable asset. Drawing upon these older catalogues as sources of examples, we can define the essential themes of catalogue content and build around them a reference framework which is valid for any collection. The objective of this grand design is to provide a structure in which the fragments of information (which are often all we have for some items in our collections) can be seen in relation to more complete records of varied affinity. At a practical level the design of the information system is such that it lends itself to adoption, optionally as a whole or in any combination of its parts, as the means of converting records from archival media and transferring them to computer.

WHAT'S IN A NAME?

Museums share the same principles and objectives as libraries, especially if we think of the great reference libraries of rare and important books. Both kinds of institution are responsible for managing an orderly collection of things that can be examined and consulted for information, for instruction and for inspiration and aesthetic satisfaction. However, unlike books in the library, the objects in a museum's collection are physically diverse and they have first to be named before they can be added to the catalogue. Certainly a librarian must compile adequate descriptions of the volumes in his care for the titles alone are quite insufficient to satisfy the inquiring reader (and more especially the literary scholar) but he is relieved of the preliminary task of naming them.

Books possess titles given by their authors and for most published works the title is a unique identifier. It is an individual name for a particular object, a name that is immutable and not amenable to alteration or susceptible to question. The title of a work of art, usually a painting or a sculpture, has the same characteristic qualities: it is the name given to it by its creator (the artist) and it is inviolable. These are the most obvious of museum objects to possess individual names but not the only ones: some products of industrial manufacture also have this rare distinction, notably locomotive engines, ships and small boats.

However, with these exceptions, a large majority of museum objects do not have individual names. Therefore to answer the question, "Does this object have a name?" or "What is the name of this object?" some thought is needed to avoid a hasty and erroneous conclusion. Not all names have the same status and anyone attempting the task of cataloguing must appreciate fully the differences disguised by the ingenuous use of the word 'name'. We have already recognised the special case in which name actually means 'title'. The question can therefore be stated in a more precise form as "Does this object have a title?". The answer is affirmative only if the object possesses a unique name conferred upon it by its creator or by its owner. Having resolved this point, we can consider what other means remain for naming objects irrespective of whether they possess titles.

The most immediate suggestion is to use the 'simple name' but on reflection it is apparent that the simple name denotes the object as a member of a group and not as a unique individual; eg 'tea-cup' is a simple name for a common article but it does not distinguish one cup among many. Curators who work with man-made objects are well aware that no general system of naming exists and certainly in their fields of collecting there is nothing comparable to the system of nomenclature available in the natural sciences.

One remaining alternative to the use of 'simple name' as a means of identifying an object is to expand it with supplementary descriptive terms which reveal the individuality of the item thus named. No doubt this is the favoured solution in many museums and it is well illustrated from the experience of a curator in a small town museum who reported as follows. "In subsequent use the short title or name of the object section at the head of the ....inventory sheet has changed its function. From using the minimum number of words possible to indicate the main characteristics of the object, it has grown into an attempt to encapsulate all the main characteristics in a single line" (J.F. Smith, 1983).

SCIENTIFIC NOMENCLATURE

The elegance of the Linnean system makes it an enviable model for all intending cataloguers to observe because it can clarify their understanding of the issues involved in naming, describing and classifying and helps to separate these three activities that are so often confused.

In the natural sciences the concept of a species unites all those individuals that are considered to be so nearly similar as to belong to the same kind. Biologists have succeeded in making this a practical and workable concept despite the intrinsic tendency of living things to exhibit individual variation resulting from genetic causes. No such difficulty arises with man-made objects and the species concept can be seen to apply equally to manufactured goods: members of a species are all those items made to the same pattern or all examples of a particular model of any article. Reverting for a moment to natural species, the biologist gives formal recognition to the existence of a species by creating and publishing a description (in Latin) and, for brief reference, by also creating and publishing a formal name (of Latin form). The description occupies at least a full paragraph and details all features that enable both comparison with and distinction from related species of closest similarity.

In the Linnean system, the two-part name or binomial is both an appellative device and also a relational device. The first part (generic name) is shared by several species of close affinity while the second part (specific epithet) is reserved in combination with the first to denote one species alone and no other. Duplicate names are not welcome and, where they have arisen, may be distinguished by the name of their author, which in every case forms an appendage to the given name.

Turning again to the world of manufactured articles, we can see that the analogy is to regard all plates made by Spode to their pattern no 1234 as constituting a species. This could be rigorously described in all material particulars and could be formally named, let us say, as 'Spode 1234'. Related ceramic wares from the same factory obviously comprise separate but related species, each having its own description and its own unique binomial appellation. Generic names might easily be found among the named decorative patterns produced by the Spode factory and specific epithets could employ the model numbers attaching to particular shapes found in the company's catalogues. Incidentally it is interesting to note that all articles from the same factory have a strong natural affinity by virtue of the composition of the porcelain, the technique used in firing, the choice of glazes and the traditions of decoration, regardless of whether they be plates, cups or teapots.

It is at once apparent that the concept of species has not been widely accepted as the basis for naming manufactured wares and, in its absence, what passes for naming is actually a kind of ecological classification. The use of common names like 'plate' and 'saucer' is not a means of naming an item with any degree of specificity. The term that we assume to be the name of the item is actually not a unique name but is the label given to an entire class of object. Who would be so bold as to offer a definition of a plate? Plates comprise an heterogeneous group of hardware objects varying in fabric, in glaze, in shape and in size;

5

not forgetting that, in addition to ceramic, they include objects made of wood, of pewter, of silver and of steel, either tinned or enamelled. Possibly the only fundamental features of all plates are their low-profile shape and their function in the serving of food.

Curators can delude themselves in thinking that they have given a specific name to an object when in reality that name is a group-name for a type of object. It has neither more nor less finality than other group names, either broader or narrower, that could be substituted. Plates can be regarded as one group within a larger community of objects (the master group) and, at the same time, comprising a number of subordinate groups to which names can be applied: for example,

master group name: tableware

group name: plate

sub-group name: bordered plate

All of these names are equally valid to reference the actual object. To name an object is to classify it, ie to label it with the name applied to other objects of that kind. It is to say, "This is a jug" (because it has the essential features possessed by all jugs). Its description, in contrast, is an identification of the individual, eg "jug of bulbous form, its rim oval and its handle taller than the body". The purpose of description is to discriminate individuals from the general population: the purpose of classification is to associate individuals into recognisable communities.

AD HOC CLASSIFICATION

Most museum catalogues have developed their conventions of usage gradually as they expanded with the continual acceptance of additional objects into the collections. This cumulative history explains why so many of the resulting classifications (so-called) are really ad hoc assemblages that have been found convenient at various times under the influence of different curators. It is common to find that, driven by expediency, a classification has been allowed to develop by adding new categories as the need for them arises. The inevitable result of this is a conglomeration of classes with variations of scale, precision and sub-division that make it clumsy and inconsistent.

6

Let costume provide an illustration here. In acquiring a varied collection of the paraphernalia of dress, it soon becomes apparent that many accoutrements are better described as Costume Accesssories than as garments. However, exactly what constitutes an accessory depends on a personal assessment of what constitutes costume. Does costume denote only the body garments or does it comprise the entire outfit of the clothed person?

In early attempts to introduce a classified approach to records of costume in the 1950's, one municipal museum soon established a dual system distinguishing Costume and Costume Accessories. In the last group were found a number of predictable categories such as shoes (or 'footwear'), shawls, scarves (or 'neckware'), stockings, gloves; --- and accoutrements including handbags, fans and parasols. However, among items included as accessories there occurred some unexpected references to garments such as shirts and underclothes (or 'underwear'), reflecting inadequacies in the two-part division that remained uncorrected through twenty years of cataloguing.

By inference these examples display a very narrow view of costume which is practically restricted to the outer garments of the torso, arms and legs. Even hats appeared to cause difficulties of decision with the result that they were sometimes treated as a group within Costume and otherwise as a group within Costume Accessories. Clearly it was left to individual intuition, on each occasion when a record was written, to assign objects to groups and to place groups within principal classes. In consequence the extra-ordinary items that were then classed among costume accessories included tennis racquet, children's dolls, hair-brush, spectacles, cigarette holder and needle case.

A classification system that has developed by "adding bits on" as each new problem presented itself is liable to consist of categories and groups that merely emphasize the haphazard ways in which solutions have been found. Because such systems are introduced in fragmented fashion, it is likely that not all of the museum's curators will be aware of the categories available for use in classification, with the result that category names are applied erratically and sometimes not at all. For example, at some stage a curator decides to create a new group within

Costume to classify ladies' swimming costumes and the general name Sportswear is coined. For no apparent reason, a tennis dress recorded by a colleague in the same year is classed simply as Costume/ Women's.

A serious disadvantage resulting from spontaneous introduction of new sub-class names is that they cannot be applied retrospectively without re-examining all existing records. With reference to the newly added category Sportswear, there are sure to be many items already catalogued that should be re-classified accordingly. In the museum providing this illustration there was, for example, an earlier record of 'riding habit' under Costume/ Women's but is this not Sportswear also?

Prompted by this last example, note that another form of variation has appeared in the naming of garments. While most of them are designated by actual garment names, eg 'dress', 'coat', 'cocked hat', some are qualified by terms indicating the context in which they were worn, ie 'riding habit', 'evening dress', 'court dress', 'wedding dress', etc. The use of social context as a descriptor of an outfit is better treated as a distinct mode of classification, not to be confused with a primary classification of garments.

Take another example from the treatment of textiles, a major class equivalent with but distinct from costume. Obviously it is a category for objects fabricated of textile material but excluding articles used as items of dress. Having made this distinction (which at first might seem to be sufficient in itself), soon it becomes apparent that some further division could be useful. Among these textiles there may be a quantity of lace handwork which it is convenient to separate from the remainder in a new sub-division named Lace. At this point it was not considered necessary to name the other textiles as a group: they are simply regarded as Textiles-excluding-Lace. Subsequently, among the residual textile materials, a significant number of 'samplers' are discovered and a sub-class of that name is established. Another sub-class founded for Tapestry at some later date is confused by a curator who introduced as an alternative name, Hangings, because it has a broader connotation and therefore accommodates a more varied range of materials. With the trend to further sub-division thus established, Embroidery is added as another sub-class under Textiles but unfortunately this has an ambi-

8

valent relation with some of the sub-classes already named (eg Samplers and Tapestry).

Having created sub-classes for these perceived groups of textiles, we are faced with the self-evident need to provide a sub-class name for every textile item, eg 'bedspread' and 'curtains'. Hence the sub-class Woven Fabrics is created as a general dump for all items not included in any of the previously mentioned groups (which are more specific). Having filed individual records for 'bedspread' and 'curtains' under the heading Woven Fabrics, it is found (perhaps predictably) that some earlier records of curtains had been classified under Hangings.

After several years of employing this pragmatic but haphazard approach to classification, the realisation becomes inescapable that the sub-classes in use are not mutually exclusive. At various times, similar objects have been classified in different ways and, in consequence, no group contains all the items it would be expected to include. Imagine the curator's dismay when it is discovered that, in breach of even the principal class boundaries, a 'lace cap' and a 'lady's jacket' have been recorded as Textiles/ Lace instead of being classed as Costume (which confusingly has sub-classes for both Lace and Headwear). Obviously, care must be taken to avoid the dispersal of similar things into unlike categories.

If curators work without reference to a formally declared set of guidelines on classification, perhaps because none has been provided, inevitably they produce records which may have individual merit but which fail to achieve the objectives of classifying. Lacking a framework of recognised class-names, curators may be left with the freedom to coin new terms as they think fitting. This has had alarming results, especially 15 to 20 years ago when the aims of classification in museums were less sophisticated and probably less clearly understood than among curators working today. The example that follows seems crude in its ineptitude but is nevertheless an actual occurrence from the catalogues of a major museum. Within a single year the same curator used three different class-names for items which he or she might have wished to relate as member objects of a group. The curator mis-construed the term Oriental, used as a class-name, possibly believing that it was a name for the region from which the object derived, eg.

4570 Oriental	4770 Far East	6570 China
Jade	Ivory	Bronze
Carving	Jewellery cabinet	Ritual vase

Actually, the choice of the geographically based name Oriental for an entire class of objects is ill-conceived, unless it defines the scope of collections for an entire department. A classification on geographical criteria is needed for all objects but should be parallel to a primary object classification, never a substitute for it. When due consideration is given to the implications of this term, it is clear that as a group designation Oriental is not equivalent to the object-based categorisk used for non-Oriental material. In other words, it accommodates a miscellany of objects which might otherwise be usefully distinguished under class-names such as Furniture, Costume, Metalwork, Glass, Ceramics, Prints and Drawings, etc. It is clear from the second terms in these examples that the bronze object qualifies for inclusion in the class Metalwork but the other two objects, ('jewellery cabinet' and 'jade carving') fall outside any of the classes mentioned up to this point. Instances of this kind are useful prompts in the formative stages of developing a classification, provoking further thought on how to accommodate objects not previously encountered.

Many classifications start off as simple two-tier structures with just one category above the object (group-) name. The class-name Furniture stands at the head of the record above the common (group-) name of the particular object, eg 'fire-screen'. However, as pieces of furniture are added to a collection in increasing variety it becomes desirable to define sub-classes containing all those pieces of a similar kind. Then the major class Furniture may have sub-classes for tables, chairs, mirrors, boxes, etc. At this stage some difficulties begin to appear. Wall mirrors and free-standing mirrors are unquestionably items of furniture but what of the small hand-mirror to be found as a toilet article on the dressing table? Does size impose some limit on what may properly be called furniture? Should we include in this class "tortoise-shell boxes inlaid with mother-of-pearl". In historical times boxes were frequently made as objects combining utility and beauty to contain hair-brushes, cosmetics, manicure and shaving requisites, jewellery, sewing materials, etc. In regard to their size and function, however, they range from personal and portable articles such as these to large and bulky objects which are indisputably items of Furniture, eg chests for the storage of linen and for safe-keeping of valuables. Clearly we have material here for an exercise in definition and, indeed, without some effort being directed towards this end the classification will remain defective. Perhaps progress might be made by drawing fundamental distinctions between furniture, implements and ornaments. By defining the practical limits to each class, the contiguous classes which surround it conceptually can be recognised, for on closer aquaintance it becomes apparent that no class exists in isolation.

As already hinted, the concept of Furniture becomes imprecise in relation to objects contributing to the decor or ornamentation of rooms. Examples include classical vases and solid urns and pedestals made of polished marble and semi-precious stone such as 'Blue John'.

These examples typify the difficulties which accompany any attempt to develop classification from a core of familiar concepts without giving thought to defining their mutual boundaries and furthest limits. They indicate that it is important, or rather essential, not merely to create a category and name it, but to define it and state its practical boundaries and the limits of its use. It is also necessary to explain what categories are relevant for objects that fall just outside the boundaries of each class, to provide sign-posts to the correct classification of things throughout the map of concepts.

VARIATION IN VOCABULARY

For anyone with the knowledge to identify museum objects the business of naming things might not seem a difficult activity. Nevertheless, to judge from the names applied to objects entered on museum record cards, for some curators the business of naming is more a projection of intuitive thoughts than a device to aid recognition of the items themselves. How else can we explain the cataloguing of three similar suits of uniform under three different names? These are (i) "Train driver's tunic"; (ii) "Transport driver's and conductor's tunic"; (iii) "Driver's and conductor's tunic" (it is not clear whether this refers to two suits or whether the two descriptions apply to the same uniform). These varied formulae of words reflect the uncertainty of the cataloguer on the most suitable name to apply. Obviously this is the cause of variation because the three uniforms are recorded under sequential numbers in the museum's register. There would be plausible excuse for the lack of conformity if they had been received separately at long intervals.

Difficulties arise from the inconsistent naming of the uniforms through the use of the words 'train' and 'transport' as alternatives for, although they must be regarded as allied terms, they are certainly not synonyms: one is more specific and the other more general. Another point that deserves to be questioned is the use of the word 'tunic' to describe a suit consisting of jacket and trousers. If the words chosen for naming are imprecise or obscure in their application to the items described then, of course, the information they convey on subsequent reading will be clouded by elements of doubt about their true identity.

The curator can easily fall into traps created by inconsistent use of words that are true synonyms, without actually noticing the fault. In a large costume collection, assembled over many years, it is common to find that women's garments are recorded under the synonyms Lady's, Ladies' and Female, while men's garments are listed as Man's, Male and even Gents. This variation could be accepted (but not approved) if it occurred in records made by curators working at different periods of time but it is a regrettable sign of idiosyncrasy to find that synonyms were written during the same year by the same team of curators. Personal preferences in nomenclature have to defer to constancy in the use of vocabulary. Only when all of these rules are observed can a series of records be considered to form a catalogue.

Changes in format appear to be minor innovations at the time when they are proposed but thought should be given to the long-term effect, especially the retrospective view of the archive already accumulated. Is it worth introducing a change of a minor character if this is at the cost of disrupting a pattern of uniformity that has prevailed in use for several decades? The practical consequences of these changes have their strongest impact at some time long after they were introduced, perhaps when attempts are made to convert the accumulated archive of catalogue records to a computer-based system.

At one institution in the course of four years the catalogues show no less than four changes of format, one of them a direct reversion to a preceding model. The disruptive effect of such erratic modification is most apparent to the user of such a catalogue, who has to re-adjust his mental orientation when reading and comparing records from year to year, frequently finding that data located according to one format does not appear in the expected place in another format. The following records illustrate the effect:

1956 Format	1957 Format	1958 Format
Costume	Coat	Cloak
Women's	Costume	Costume
Date acquired	Men's	Women's
Donor	English	English
Value	Date acquired	Date of origin
Dress	Donor	Date acquired
English	Value	Donor
	Date of origin	Value
	Description	Description

Before any changes are brought into effect, it is obvious that all requirements should be thoroughly analysed to discover what information should contribute to the record and how it should be arranged. Actually a period of experiment can be justified to conduct trials using various models of record composition and format. Eventually, when decisions have been taken and the chosen model has been implemented it should be a prime concern to maintain stability in all aspects of the structure of records and to avoid deviation from the established pattern and practice. Indeed, if it be thought essential subsequently to make any change in the record structure, it must be implied that all previous catalogue entries shall be re-written to the new standard.

SUMMARY

In the first half of this century museum objects were catalogued by their common names without any thought of indicating their membership of a broader category. (Thus we find objects named 'snuff-box', 'flute', 'chair', 'knife', etc). This practice continues up to the present day in departments which have consistently avoided the prospect of introducing a classification. Two difficulties are inherent in the resulting catalogues which severely limit their capabilities as information resources. Firstly, there is no control over the application of names to objects and consequently curators catalogue similar items under different names, eg 'relief fragment' and 'stele fragment'. This syndrome is typified as "one class by many names". Conversely, over a period of years, some names are applied to a wider range of objects than was at first intended: this is characterised as "many objects by one name".

Secondly, the lack of any group name to designate the general class to which the object belongs, makes it impossible to relate items in ways that might be useful to the collection manager. For example, two items named as 'figurine' and 'wooden head' respectively could with benefit share a suitable group name of a higher order: possibly in this case the name might be 'effigy'. As an aid to searches in a catalogue broader classes of this kind are invaluable: how else can we discover the existence of objects named only as 'butter-hand', 'palstave' and 'fleam'?

Almost as bad as a catalogue with no classification is a catalogue classified by ad hoc procedures. This mis-guided practice appeared in many institutions during the last thirty years, presumably as a hasty remedy for the previous absence of classification. Categories were devised to meet the need for a group name in individual cases as they occurred (if only to fill the space on the first line of the record). If an object could not be accommodated in one of the categories already existing, then a new class had to be created. One predictable consequence of this approach is that there is uncertainty about the correct assignment of objects to classes. For example, 'autograph letter' is in some cases classed under Manuscripts while a similar item is found under Documents. Alternatively it is classed under both categories because they are not mutually exclusive, with cross-reference from one to the other. Variation in the spelling of class names (singular, plural and even in abbreviated form) adds further confusion.

A final problem occurs when attempts are made to improve defective classifications: the improvement cannot be effected only in the on-going catalogue but must be introduced retrospectively as well. Otherwise the difficulties are compounded by the co-existence of incompatible systems of nomenclature (the old and the new) or of similar terms representing different levels of hierarchy before and after the revision.

Despite a general awareness of inadequacies in the past treatment of names, both simple and classifed, there is considerable inertia in the attitude adopted to the question of improvement, as shown by Brears (1984) in the following remarks.

"In an attempt to bring some kind of order into an increasingly confused and disparate situation (ie concerning social history classifications) the Group for Regional Studies in Museums held a one-day conference on classification at Birmingham Museum in 1978. Instead of producing a unanimous call for a standard system, however, the meeting clearly illustrated that many curators saw no advantage in classifying their collections, while others knew that their own system was perfect for their purposes and needed no improvement."

The fact that fundamental principles of a seemingly obvious kind need detailed exposition here is not entirely a reflection on present standards of competence in museums. It is, however, necessary on the grounds that modern curators often discover that the record systems they take over from previous incumbents are defective in one way or another. This situation is largely a consequence of institutional histories and of the idiosyncrasies of museum keepers in earlier decades when amateurs and enthusiasts were entrusted with tasks now seen to be of a professional nature. None of the examples in this book are fictitious: they are real and it is axiomatic that most curators experience difficulties with existing documentation which approximate to those examined in this and the following chapters.

15

REFERENCES

Brears, P. (1984)   "SHIC: genesis." MDA Information vol.8 no.2 p.30.

Smith, J.F. (1983) "Stamford Museum." MDA Information vol.6 no.4 p.63.

Chapter 2

Textual records

For many museums with a long history, the strengths and weaknesses of textual records will be thoroughly familiar. However, curators not yet acquainted with the benefits and impediments of previous document-ation may find the very idea of textual records incongruous. For them and for entrants to the profession, a critical look at the phenomenon can be an invaluable preparation for the practical business of writing structured records. Museums which possess documentation of collections in the form of textual records face a major problem when considering how these can be prepared for entry to computerised information systems. Not only does the issue raise many questions about the means of converting data held in this form but the sheer bulk and volume of such archives impose a task whose magnitude is itself a formidable problem. For a century-old museum, these records can comprise more than half of the total documentary archive.

WHAT ARE TEXTUAL RECORDS?
They are records in registers and catalogues written in narrative prose which is not methodically structured in a consistent fashion. There may be a detectable style in presentation but it does not conform to a regular pattern: textual records lack internal organisation. Components of information, whether observed or reported, do not correspond from

17

one record to the next in respect of what is included and what omitted. Textual records are infinitely variable in what information they contain and how it is expressed: the resultant lack of comparability is frustrating and yet, at the same time, it is fascinating to discover in them a wealth of eclectic detail.

One of the most beneficial results of studying textual catalogues is to discover the extent of information that is potentially available for all objects and the relation between the information and the object itself. Some information is the result of direct observation (which can be repeated by any observer) while other data is acquired knowledge that has been received as written or spoken statement from some other source, perhaps a former owner for example. There can be no broader basis for discovering the range of information that is available about museum objects because in textual records this information is presented entirely free from constraint.

The fact that records are textual does not itself indicate whether the information they contain is adequate or inadequate: the shortest of textual records is as inadequate as the shortest of structured records. The following examples make the point:

606   Soup Tureen. Round, gadroon, with liner.

608   Vegetable Dish 12". Round, gadroon, with partitions.

611   Breakfast Dish and Warmer. Shell and flower mounts.
         Mark: 2 stars. L. 15½" W. 10½"

These are the simplest of unstructured records as found in ordinary sale-room catalogues. Note that dimensions are given sometimes but not in every case. When included, measurement is stated at any convenient point and not in a consistent position where its presence could be anticipated.

Textual records are commonly found in registers in which an entry was made for each object as a record of its acquisition at the time of its receipt. Because items were entered (and numbered) in chronologic order, on occasions when several objects were received from the same donor, it was usual to write a statement on the circumstances of acquisition as a discrete paragraph of narrative text preceding the records to which it refers, eg

18

"The following dies, for buttons, badges, etc made by Dowler, Birmingham including a lead impression from each die, were presented by Messrs. William Dowler & Sons, Ltd. 1936."

"The following items, worn by Miss Catharine Ellen Parkes at her wedding to Thomas Roderick in 1854, were presented by Miss Florence Parkes, niece of the wearer."

Incorporated into these statements there is supplementary information which in principle relates to every one of the ensuing object records. Individual records which are members of such series do not repeat these data concerning their acquisition and consequently, if read in isolation, they may appear to be deficient in some essential details.

It is now appropriate to examine some typical examples of narrative records to appreciate their variable content and style:

Example 1   (Fine Art)

Volume of Five Sepia Drawings after Cotman (1782-1842) lithographed by Vincent Brooks, Day and Son, London; 1882. For use of schools in connection with the Board of Trade Department of Science and Art. The subjects of the lithographs are as follow: "Chapel of St.Quentin of the Rock", "Castle and Port of Granville", "Lyons", "Perriers near Domfront", "Exterior of a Church with Romanesque doorway".

Although it imparts quite substantial information about the item, this is an unsatisfactory record by present standards. Dimensions are not given, nor are details of the cover and binding of the volume (by which it might be more easily recognised). The position of the titles of the individual plates and of the volume itself is not stated. There is an interesting reference to an Association with the "Department of Science and Art" but its exact significance is not clear.

Example 2   (Applied Art)

Bowl, circular, on four feet. Silver, repousse and chased, the decoration being done with punches and chisels. Round the body a band of ornament consisting of ogee-headed panels containing stylised foliage and flowers, separated by ribs terminating in

19

points; above and below is a frieze with trefoil ornament, which also occurs on the boss-shaped feet. Malay; about 1770.

This record contains useful reference to the Technique that produced the ornamentation and it gives details of the Decoration but omits to mention the form of the bowl itself (ie its proportions). The size of the bowl is not revealed by any measurement: weight is a practical characteristic to record for any item of precious metalwork.

Example 3   (Mechanical Instrument)

Watch, with paired cases. The outer case covered with a thin disc of shell or horn, its underside painted in colours with shepherdess and sheep in a landscape. The inner case of gilt metal containing movement with verge escapement, of gilt metal, with pierced and engraved cock with solid foot, and plain cylindrical pillars. White enamel dial, with plain gold hour and minute hands. Back-plate engraved with name of maker and place of manufacture:
"Wm. Beavington, Stourbridge. 74984". The cases bear the maker's mark: "N.T.W.". English (Stourbridge); late 18th or early 19thC. Inside the outer case are watch papers of Dumbell, Watch & Clock Maker, of Bilston St., Wolverhampton; and of Blurton, Watch & Clock Maker, Stourbridge.

The strengths of this record are the rigorous description of the watch's construction and the very clear statements on the presence of Makers' Marks (inscribed names, etc) for both mechanism and watchcases. Interestingly, it establishes the object's Association with local horological trades by recording the papers found inside the outer case.

Example 4   (Costume)

Wedding Dress. Blue silk; combined bodice and skirt. Full skirt for crinoline with two deep flounces and fine pierced scalloped edging. High necked bodice with wide elbow length sleeves and net insets, trimmed with pink silk ribbon. Epaulette shoulder, tunic front and V-shaped back; trimmed with blue and white fringe a loose belt and hanging for the back. Worn by Miss Field on her marriage in 1848 to Mr. John Driver of Stroud, Gloucestershire, who later moved to Birmingham where he kept a public house and museum in Highgate Place.

Certainly this account provides information on the style, as well as the fabric and the colour of the dress. It is a serviceable record rather than a complete one: it would enable the dress to be recognised among a collection of several or many but it would not stand alone as a literal description of the costume. In particular, references to trimmings with "pink silk ribbon" and "blue and white fringe" do not make clear their position on the garment. No mention is made of the form of collar. It must be supposed that the belt and "hanging" are of matching fabric. Reference to the V-shaped back is a little obscure. In the following sentence we note there is information on circumstances associated with the wedding, ie its date and the name of the bridegroom. This statement then extends to mention some biographical facts about him which cannot logically contribute to the cataloguing of the dress.

The free-form style of textual records allows them to be expanded to incorporate all kinds of incidental information which enlarges the knowledge available about an object. The disadvantage, of course, is that as the text increases to beyond the size of a normal paragraph, it becomes a cumbersome vehicle for information. The absence of internal structure and headings leave no alternative to the reader but to study the whole narrative in order to discover what elements of information it contains. We now examine some examples that display these characteristics and which also contain interesting aspects of description.

Example 5   (Local History)

Sailmaker's Bench of wood, padded, at one end a bag for tools and holes for tools; with needles, tools and a piece of sail, from the Stourport Docks of the Severn and Worcester Canal Carrying Company. The bench was usually placed in the centre of a large room known as the sailmaker's loft.   The tools comprise:

1.   Serving Mallet for rope rigging;

2.   Small Rope Mallet used exclusively for wire rope;

3.   Marline Spike, of wood, used for splicing;

21

4. Fid, of steel, used for splicing the larger sections of coir and limp rope;

5. Fid, of wood, the type used for splicing ropes 100 years ago, replaced by more modern metal type similar to No.4;

6. Stabber for making holes in canvas for inserting rings or eyelets;

7. Gauge (similar to carpenter's gauge) for marking width of seams on canvas;

8. Hook and Line used for keeping canvas taut across sailmaker's knees when sewing seams;

9. Goose or Rubbers for flattening round canvas seams: wooden type of Norwegian origin. It was superseded by a metal type, which gives greater pressure;

10. Palm Needle and Beeswax;

11. Sailmaker's Twine Winder;

    Together with the tools are a Sailmaker's Canvas Tool-bag; and a Piece of Canvas used for sailmaking.

Here we are dealing with an object (or suite of objects) created solely for the practical purposes of industrial use in sailmaking. The maker of the sailmaker's bench and tools is not stated and is perhaps not of prime concern (though usually the original manufacturer of any object is required data). However, the place where the equipment was used, "the Stourport Docks" is reported; together with the name of the firm that operated it, "the Severn and Worcester Canal Carrying Company". Then follows a statement which is probably superfluous, relating to the usual location of such tools in the "sailmaker's loft". This would have no place in a structured record in its present form but could be added as the exact site within the company's premises. At several places in this record there are remarks that would be more appropriate in the text of a display label explaining the derivation and development of the tools on exhibition; eg "The wooden type is of Norwegian origin" and "replaced by more modern metal type similar to No.4". These phrases are not elements of literal description but pieces of circumstantial information whose inclusion in the formal record may be questioned. Lastly, but not least, the record of tools used on the bench mentions the

Function of each item. This element of catalogue data is relevant in describing all implements of craft and industry.

Example 6   (Local History)

Wooden Paddle of unknown function. Carved from a single piece of oak; blade tapered into rounded handle with short cross T-arms at the top. Total length 45 cm. Back surface is slightly convex and tapers down towards each side but not to the bottom end. Sides of object considerably bruised and broken. Object was found during construction work on the moated site of Rugeley Manor House and could be of quite considerable antiquity. The Manor House is situated in Armitage, about half a mile from the Church. Suggestions as to its use include a thatcher's bat, an oven peel and a flax-dressing bat or washing bat.

Here we have an object which cannot be given a definitive name because its purpose has not been recognised. It is fortunate therefore, that the record provides a thorough Description which would readily identify the object within a collection. Another facet of information commonly encountered with objects that were lost, abandoned or buried is the location of the find-spot. This place-name is the most significant data we have concerning this object. Unfortunately, in this case, we do not know exactly at what position on the site the object was discovered, ie was it found actually in the moat? Such information, relating to the Environment of the find, is of the greatest importance in recording historical and archaeological objects.

Example 7   (Archaeology)

Stone Slab incised with cuneiform inscription. From the Temple of Nabu at Nineveh, erected by Ashurbanipal in the third quarter of the 7th century BC. The Temple of Nabu was re-discovered in 1904 and finally cleared in 1927-8, the excavations being carried out by Dr. R. Campbell Thompson and others. The following is a translation of the inscription:-

"Unto Nabu, the supreme Lord dwelling in E.Zida, which is in the middle of Nineveh, his lord Ashurbanipal, King of Assyria, the one sought after and desired by his great divinity, who at the utterance of his behest and the giving of his weighty ordinance, in the shock of battle cut off the head of Teumman, King of Elam, and, as for Ummanigash, Tammaritu, Pa'e, Ummanaldas, who after Teumman ruled over Elam, by his great command my hand captured them and unto the wagon, vehicle of my majesty, I yoked them. By his great aid throughout all lands I secured what was due to me. In those days, my Lord, the court of the Temple of Nabu with solid limestone its area I enlarged. For all time, O Nabu, look with joy (thereon) and may it be pleasing unto thee by thy ruled line. May thine ordinance go forth that my feet be long to tread E.Zida before thy presence."

The apparent wealth of information in this record disguises the fact that there is remarkably little physical description of the object itself. The consequence is that it could prove difficult to identify this stone among a number of others bearing cuneiform inscriptions. There is no mention of the outline shape of the slab nor of any distinguishing marks (even defects). The cataloguer was engrossed in the social and religious significance of the stone in its original context to the exclusion of mundane requirements.

As with the sailmaker's bench, here too the actual maker of the object (the stone-mason) is not known but the name of the Assyrian king who commanded its creation is known. The term 'maker' might be loosely interpreted to admit the name "Ashurbanipal" but more correctly this personage might be regarded as important by Association. Other data of a kind which occurs regularly in connection with archaeological objects relates to the place and circumstances of Discovery. The only place-name given is the location where the stone was originally sited ("the Temple of Nabu at Nineveh") and where it was subsequently discovered by excavation. Details ancillary to this situation include the dates of discovery and excavation and the name of the 'finder' (in this case, the excavator). The greater part of the record consists in a translation of the Inscription and this emphasises the necessity for records that are unrestricted in length.

24

Example 8   (Arms and Armour)

Broadsword; steel with pierced basket hilt. The blade inscribed "Thomas Gill Birmingham 1790. Manufacture of England. Warranted Never to Fail". English (Birmingham); dated 1790. Made by Thomas Gill, of Jennens' Row, Birmingham who made great efforts to improve the quality of sword-cutlery in England. Consequent on a petition by London cutlers to be allowed to import German blades free of duty, he memorialised the Lords of the Treasury in 1783 to the effect that he could make as good if not better blades than the Germans. In 1796 a trial took place using a machine invented by Matthew Boulton, of 10,000 blades ordered by the East India Company. Of 1400 German blades 28 were rejected. Of Gill's 2650 blades only 4 failed to pass the test. 1,084 of the British blades other than Gill's were rejected. Among Gill's other activities, he supplied springs for a flying machine invented by the Scotsman Miller. [Information supplied by J.G.Mann, keeper of the Wallace Collection, in a letter 30th Dec. 1937] See also article on Gill in "Connoisseur", July 1927. Purchased at £6 from Messrs. Fenton & Sons, Ltd., 33 Cranbourn Street, Leicester Square, London W.C.1.

Once again we have a record that gives little attention to the physical description of the object but at least the sword can be identified from the maker's inscription (which is quoted). Neither dimensions nor the form of the blade are reported and no distinctive features of the hilt or basket are described. The stature of Gill as a master cutler is well borne out by the account of competitive testing of his swords against those of other English and also German makers. Clearly the inclusion of this narrative is justified by reference to the inscription "Warranted Never to Fail". Nevertheless, on strict analysis this must be regarded as circumstantial information and not an essential part of a catalogue record: it would be entirely apt in an exhibition label. However, we should not overlook the references made to Matthew Boulton and to the East India Company, both of which have a legitimate place in the record by their Association with the object. In the same category also is the name of the Scottish inventor, Miller. Lastly, the record cites sources

25

for information both published and unpublished: such Citations have a proper place in catalogue records that are claimed to be comprehensive.

Example 9   (Fine Art)

William Hogarth (1697-1764), oil on canvas, "The Distressed Poet". Date 1735. Collection of the Duke of Westminster. Given by the artist to Mrs. Draper, Queen Caroline's midwife, and at her death sold for £5. 5s. 0d. to a solicitor named Ward, from whom it was purchased for £14. 14s. 0d. by the first Earl Grosvenor, in the possession of whose family it has always remained.

The most likely theory concerning the subject of this picture is that it was inspired by the plight of Lewis Theobald, the poet described by Pope in "Dunciad", for beneath the first engraving of the picture four lines from that work are quoted by Hogarth, thus: "Studious he sat........etc
Exhibited: B.I.1814, no.100; B.I.1824, no.144; B.I.1841,no.85; R.A 1871, no.228; Burlington Fine Arts Club 1871, no.31; Grosvenor Gallery 1888, no.29. Engraved by Hogarth, published (first state) March 3rd, 1736. See "William Hogarth" by Austin Dobson, 1898, pp 57, 67-9, 230, 295. Reproduced in the "Times", 2nd August, 1934; the "Times Weekly Edition", 9th August, 1934; "Illustrated London News", 4th August, 1934.

The record of this picture follows the tradition among art curators of cataloguing the object under the name of the artist instead of by its title (which is the unique identifier). For the purposes of a curator of paintings, the artist's name is used in an idiosyncratic sense as a term of classification. Appended to the artist's name are the years of his birth and death, which place him into historical context. In cases when two persons bear the same name (eg father and son), these 'life-dates' may help to identify the individual.

There follows an account of the sequence of Ownership from the origin of the painting down to its acquisition by the museum. This history of owners is considered important by art historians and, as every owner in turn holds the same relation to the object which he possesses, the record of all known owners is properly included in a complete catalogue. The second paragraph propounds a "theory concerning the subject of this picture", relating to interpretation of the image, which is more appropriate to an exhibition catalogue than to a curatorial record. Except for the phrase "oil on canvas", there is virtually no attempt to describe the physical attributes of the picture; for example, its size, frame, stretcher, identity marks and labels, etc.

The list of Exhibitions in which the picture has been shown forms the last part of this record and, like Ownerships, being part of the object's history it is usually considered relevant to a catalogue for works of fine art. Why it is not equally relevant for works of archaeological antiquity or industrial manufacture is an elusive question. Another feature that is peculiar to picture records is to mention Reproductions of the work, eg as engravings or as copies.

Example 10   (Fine Art)

Meindert Hobbema (1638-1709), oil on wood panel,'The Water Mill'. Signed 'M. Hobbema'. Certified as work by Hobbema by Dr. Gluck, the Vienna Kunst-historischesmuseum; by Dr. Hofstede de Groote and by Director of the Hals Museum, Haarlem. In his certificate dated 7th April 1931 Dr. Gluck writes on the back of a photograph of the painting:

"The picture on oak, 67.5cm high by 97cm broad, was known to me by personal inspection and close study. I consider it to be important and distinguished by reason of the noble sentiments ("Stimmung") with which it is imbued, and also because of its careful execution. It is a genuine and characteristic work of Meindert Hobbema, of his mature period. The picture is signed in the lower left corner with the name of the painter. The same water-mill is represented by Hobbema in two pictures belonging to the Rijksmuseum at Amsterdam, in two different views on a larger scale. It also appears in other landscapes, eg that in the Wallace Collection in London." (translated from the German).

Hofstede de Groote, in a certificate dated June 1928, states that he considers it to be a "genuine and a characteristic work by Meindert Hobbema, fully signed in the lower left corner".

The Director of the Frans Hals Museum at Haarlem also certified the painting in a written declaration dated 23/11/1931, in which he "considers it to be a very beautiful and characteristic work by Meindert Hobbema of his best time" (expressed in original English). The Water Mill, shown in the above painting, re-appears seen from nearly the same point of view (from the front left-hand corner) in No.99 at the Wallace Collection (No.85 in volume IV of De Groot's "Catalogue of Dutch Painters", under Hobbema); in No.1188 at the Rijksmuseum, Amsterdam (De Groot, No.67); No.16 at the Chicago Art Institute (De Groot, No.71). It also is represented, from other points of view, in No.1187 at the Rijksmuseum (De Groot, No.66) and in No.220 at the Brussels Museum (De Groot, No.69); also by De Groot Nos. 75, 81 and 86.

Purchased by the donors for £x000 from Messrs. Brown, of Duke Street, St. James's, London. Presented by Trustees of the John Feeney Charitable Bequest, on the Centenary of the Borough.

The wealth of information given here contains the full text of three testimonial statements by independent authorities on the Attribution of the work to the artist Hobbema. This aptly illustrates the need for provision to be made in structured records for the considered opinion of experts on the validity of the object (or of the name applied to it). There is no means of curtailing the length of such statements if they are recorded <u>verbatim</u>. Even when given in reported form, it is essential to name the author (of the opinion), his place of work or affiliation, the date and substance of his testimony. In critical vein, it must be noticed that apart from the particulars in quoted statements, the record displays almost total lack of physical description of the object itself, its markings, defects if any and general condition. A feature of interest is the paragraph listing other works which treat the identical water-mill as their subject: these are related images and therefore should be classed as Associated Works.

Example 11   (Applied Art)

Design for a Stained Glass Window in Bedford Parish Church. Pencil and watercolour drawing for a 4-light and tracery window.

Tracery has IHS in sun rays centrally divided by a mullion, an open book and (..?) <u>dexter</u>, an anvil and dove above a tabernacle <u>sinister</u>, motifs in yellow with background of pale blues, pinks and yellows, with four deep blue quatrefoil traceries. Below, the date 1552 in a gold circle with wreath, an heraldic eagle wings outstretched and ribbon scroll above and below, the lower inscribed "Dame Alice Harpur School". In black script below against background of pale greens, pinks, blues and yellows : "PRAISE GOD/ for the generous/ exertions of/ SIR WILLIAM/ HARPUR/ and of/ DAME ALICE/ his wife/ in bringing/ the Light of/ Learning to the SERVANTS OF GOD." Below a ribbon scroll inscribed "Bedford Modern" and a red heraldic eagle, wings outstretched.

The second light has the red cross arms of the City of London in a gold wreath, ribbon scroll inscribed "LONDON" and semi-circular arch below which stand an Elizabethan Gentleman in red robe holding a flaming torch. Below are arms with harp supporters and lettering "SIR WILLIAM HARPUR".

The third light has heraldic black eagle wings outstretched with "BEDFORD" on ribbon scroll below, an Elizabethan Woman with green mantle and blue-purple dress holding a flaming torch below a semi-circular arch. Arms and harp supporters below with lettering "DAME ALICE HIS WIFE".

The sinister light has a wreathed medallion dated '1975', and a black eagle wings outstretched between ribbon scrolls, the lower inscribed "BEDFORD SCHOOL". As a mirror to it, the dexter light, lettering "MAY GOD/ prosper the/ continuance/ of their endeavour/ in the four/ schools still/ assisted by/ their bounty/ administered/ through the/ HARPUR TRUST", has a blue eagle wings outstretched under ribbon scroll inscribed "BEDFORD HIGH". The cartoons for this window form part of the Brian Thomas Gift. The window was commissioned by The Harpur Trust of Bedford, a charity devoted to education.

The descriptive part of this record is in narrative form, extending to four or five paragraphs, and it displays considerable complexity. This might be regarded as a vindication of the textual method of recording, for how else could such detail be presented? Its peculiarity is the intimate association of images and inscriptions, two elements of information that are normally segregated in a structured record. However, it can be challenged on failing to convey its content clearly; indeed, even after a second reading some doubts remain about the relative positions of various images and inscriptions. In striving to state every point of detail, the overall design is lost to the reader. The intricacies of positional information, (eg "In black script below.."; "above tabarnacle sinister ...") create the impression of reading a legal document. The relationship between one image or inscription and another is concealed by the ponderous form of expression. In reality, this example may be the most persuasive demonstration of the defects of narrative text and of reasons for developing a structured alternative.

Example 12   (Applied Art)

Tapestry Panel, depicting a Unicorn Hunt. Woven in coloured wools, blues and greens predominating, reds faded. In the centre a unicorn being attacked with spears by five men, two of them on horseback. The unicorn is thrusting his horn against one of them on the left. A second unicorn appears beneath the horse on the right. In the middle distance a third unicorn is being fired at with a pistol by a horseman on the left, who is balanced on the right by another horseman, also firing at the same unicorn. Landscape background with trees, buildings and mountains. Tulips and other flowers in foreground. Border (repaired) of fruit, flowers, birds and animals. Flemish; about 1630.

Collection of Sir William Burrell, Hutton Castle, Berwick-on-Tweed, from whom it was bought as a special concession to the Art Gallery for the sum of £x000, which was remitted, at Sir William Burrell's instructions, to the Red Cross Sale at Christie's.

Presented 1940 through The Association of Friends of the Gallery through the generosity of the following subscribers:- Aaron Nash, Alderman W A Hadbury, Edward Grey, and an Anonymous Donor."

The absence of a known title, such as a picture would have, provides some reason why the tapestry is described in terms of the images it

30

contains, yet the picture by Hobbema was not detailed by scrutiny of this kind. Pictorial representation, ie the subject matter of Imagery is usually of great interest to museum visitors and therefore is a subject of proper concern for curators. Unfortunately in this case it is treated at considerable length to the exclusion of purely material description, which is very sparse. The casual mention of repair made to the border of the hanging is inadequate for a feature of such importance to the curator: it should be expanded to indicate the size of area repaired and its precise location on the tapestry. Overall dimensions of the tapestry are not given and this omission must cause practical difficulties for the curator planning to display it.

As this example shows, terms of Acquisition can be quite complex: several individuals and organisations may be mentioned in the credits. Acknowledgments here include the name of the vendor, who was himself a benefactor in selling the tapestry at a concessionary price, as well as the names of four subscribers who met this cost, acting as instruments of the Association of Friends (also to be acknowledged). In the final analysis, the tapestry was actually 'presented' to the museum as a gift but the agency of all those involved in securing its acquisition requires due mention.

Example 13   (Local History)

Knife, Fork and Bodkin in leather case.

The set is believed to have belonged to John Lewis Burckhardt (1784-1817) the Swiss explorer. The knife has ivory strips on one side of the handle engraved with the figure of St. Joseph holding the infant Christ; on the other side of handle is an inscription in German handschrift. The blade bears a German inscription on both sides. On the fork, the ivory strip on one side of the handle is engraved with the figure of St. James; on the other side is an inscription in German handschrift. On the bodkin, the ivory strips on both sides of the handle are engraved with a foliage design. Overall length in case: 9 inches. 17th century.

The preceding record, like those already discussed, is deficient in accurate physical description (especially of the number of ivory strips affixed to the handles and the means of their attachment). Individual dimensions of the three pieces are not reported nor is the form of construction and closure of the case. However, the record concentrates on two aspects: the Association with the Swiss explorer, Burckhardt, and the presence of Inscriptions. Although we are told that the several inscriptions are in the German language and their positions are made clear, it is surprising that no text is given either in the original or else in translation.

Example 14   (Local History)

A jug commemorating in verse (i) the Duke of Wellington and (ii) the Boxer of Birmingham Town.

Pottery, white fabric, light blue glaze, painted decoration; c.1810. Provenance unknown.   Height c. 19 cm.

Decorated on one side with portrait of Wellington and below it the following lines:

>"We'll drink success to Wellington,
>The valiant hero's name,
>Victorious deeds he has perform'd
>So mighty is his fame.
>His Army and the Navy join
>In universal cheer,
>Their gallantry let us resound
>And shout in every ear."

On the other side a pattern of leaves and grapes and below this the following verses:

>Sam Scott the fly boatman a chap of renown
>Beat Granby the boxer of Birmingham Town.
>He beat him so much with his great clumsey fist
>That poor Granby the boxer could scarcely exist.

>It was on a large common near Moseley Wake Green
>The combatants met to and were plain to be seen.
>The first setting to it was not much amiss
>But Sam made poor Granby near ready to p-s.

[three more verses of similar length intervene before concluding .....]

> So this was the way that the battle was ended
> I think that poor Granby was not much befriended
> For instead as expected to have beaten bold Scott,
> To Sam's satisfaction it was his own lot.

Clearly, from experience with previous examples, there is insufficient information in this record to describe the object adequately, particularly in regard to the form of the jug, its lip and its handle. The colour of the painted decoration is not stated. What is remarkable, however, is the length of its commemorative Inscriptions, which are quoted in full, creating difficulties for the storage of documentation.

This is a problem that has to be considered and resolved in whatever manner is thought suitable by each museum for its own purposes. Some will insist that it is correct and necessary to record the verses in full as a matter of principle, arguing that this is not an exceptional case but one which is perhaps only a little longer than the inscriptions on some other objects for which full-length records were made. Is there at any point a limit to what should be accepted in the record when reporting the visible features of a piece? If it be argued that a simple reference to the subject of the inscription is sufficient, it might be advisable to record some keywords of particular interest taken from the verses, such as mention of place-names, eg Moseley Wake Green.

The inherent weakness of textual records is their tendency to be unbalanced, in so far as one or two features of the object may be treated in detail and at some length while other aspects may be overlooked. Probably this occurs as a consequence of the deflection of the cataloguer's interest to those features of obvious appeal or rarity. A text record is, in origin, a scholarly essay which is not intended nor well suited for the purposes of information retrieval. In the absence of a template there are no prompts to alert the writer of text records to all the particulars that may have relevance for a curator and which may serve in future to aid comparisons not yet foreseen.

Chapter 3

Structured records

DEFINITION AND CHARACTERISTICS

At some stage in the development of its record procedures, every museum has attempted, with varying degrees of achievement, to organise the content of object records into a form having recognisable structure. This structure shows its presence in two related aspects affecting the presentation of information. The fundamental feature is the regular treatment of salient facts in a pre-determined sequence, consistently applied to all records in a file. A more obvious but superficial feature is the arrangement of statements in a planned lay-out ('format') on the card or page.

The essential characteristic of a structured record is the segmentation of its content into 'elements' that follow one another in predictable order. Elements are parts of statements, each of which records a particular attribute of the object, for example the material of which it is made, its dimensions, its decoration; or facts concerning its history, such as the name of its last owner. The development of structure aids rapid comparison between corresponding elements of successive records, something which is axiomatic in modern thinking but which was almost impossible with older textual records.

The most noticeable feature of the first attempts to write records in structured form is the limited extent of their factual content, both in concept and in mode of expression. It should be made clear, therefore, that neither brevity nor restriction of the concepts treated is inherently necessary in creating structured records. In fact, there is even less reason now for such limitations, using computers to manipulate records, than when using typescript pages or cards. The initial simplification of records was perhaps a reaction to the lengthy and ill-defined formats that were previously accepted. At their first introduction, the reduced content of structured records represented what was perceived as being all the information that could be standardised. No one, today, should suppose that a structured record requires all its elements to be reduced to minimal proportions or that they must be phrased to fit a formula. If brevity and conformity are regarded as paramount objectives the consequence can easily be to distort information and degrade the quality of the record.

EARLY EXAMPLES OF STRUCTURE

The first tentative steps made in this direction by many museums were cautious and the early products of documentation in structured form are in striking contrast to the diffuse texts of narrative records by reason of their brevity. There was evidently a desire to simplify the content of statements, to reduce their diversity and make it easier to read records at a glance by formatting their arrangement. The effect of structuring makes it easier to inspect records held on index cards because the pertinent information is displayed in standardised arrangement and hence occurs in a predictable position on the card. Then it is possible to view and quickly to compare data in any desired element.

This process of comparison is even more effective when carried out by automated methods and that is the reason which motivates a majority of those museums that are now converting their record management to computer. However, these considerations can be better appreciated after looking at the simpler situation represented in the card-index model used throughout the past several decades. Some quite simple examples, taken from museum archives soon after the first introduction of structured records, illustrate the fundamental features of this treatment.

Example 15   Drawing
               By Louise M Baker
               c. 1923
               Watercolour on paper
               Painting of mosaic inlay of chest 10441
               Published as Plate 94 Excavations at Ur, volume 2
               Insurance value £x.00

Example 16   Floor-tile
               From Nottingham
               Purchased from the executors of E G Champion
               14th and 15th century
               Shield, a lion rampant reversed
               Pattern no. 17 in Trans. Thornton Soc. vol 36 p.90
               Insurance value: part of £x.00

Example 17   Medal commemorating accession of Queen Anne
               8th March 1702
               English
               John Croker
               Silver
               Insurance value £x.00

Example 18   Teapot
               Ceramics
               Pottery
               Soft paste
               English   ?Castleford
               early 19th century
               received April 1957
               presented anonymously
               Value £x.00
               Height to knop: 6 inches
               White half-glossy stoneware, fluted body and spout.
               Applied decoration of festoons and acanthus leaves.

36

Structure is apparent in the separation of phrases relating to the different elements of information: this is emphasised by the format in which each element is placed on a new line. The first thing to notice is that the number of elements comprising each record is variable.

These four records have several elements in common: they include a name for the object, a date (of its origin) and an insurance value. A description of visible features and of the material of which the object was made are not universally present in early examples of structured records. The tentative and experimental nature of these first attempts is evident in Examples 15-18.

The presence or absence of some elements is dictated by decisions on whether information exists and on its relevance if it is obtainable. For example, the illustrator who created the drawing is named, as also is the maker of the medal, but no comparable information exists for the manufacturer of the teapot or the floor-tile. However, the place where each of these latter items was manufactured is given but, in contrast, the place where the drawing was made is presumed irrelevant and the place where the medal was cast is not known (except to class it as English).

Within the records of the archaeological drawing and the floor-tile there is reference to the publication in which that item was illustrated but there is no equivalent reference for the medal and the teapot, either because no illustration was ever made or because the cataloguer was not aware of it.

It might seem anomalous that only two of these examples include a statement on the museum's acquisition of the objects, ie the floor-tile "purchased from the executors", the teapot "presented anonymously". The explanation lies in the fact that the drawing was one of a series received from the same source as a single gift and its acquisition was reported in a general statement entered in the register as a paragraph preceding the catalogue of individual records. This states that "The following drawings are the original illustrations made by Louise Baker of objects from Ur presented by Sir Leonard Woolley at an unknown date". A comparable statement precedes the series of over 200 medals which were purchased as an entire private collection. This record of acquisition was not reproduced when copying individual records onto cards.

When each of these diverse records (Examples 15 - 18) is seen in comparison with others describing objects of the same kind, then a more consistent pattern emerges. Viewed in the context of the numismatic catalogue, the record for the Queen Anne medal (Example 17) repeats the structure and format used consistently for the entire collection of medals. Similarly, the catalogue cards for ceramics demonstrate a consistent structure and format appropriate to data on that material. Inevitably the archaeological catalogue includes a greater variety of objects and as with all heterogeneous collections, exhibits greater variation in record structure.

Among the examples so far considered, only one of the structured records is also seen to be classified (ie the teapot): there is no general implication that structured records are necessarily classified and it is important to avoid confusion on this point. On closer inspection, it is seen that differences occur in the treatment of data within elements: the naming of objects is a case in point. A single word is used as a definitive term to name an item in the records relating to the 'drawing', 'floor-tile' and 'teapot'. In contrast, the term 'medal' is augmented by a unique phrase which identifies the particular subject of this record in distinction from all others (except its replicates). It is named "Medal commemorating (the) accession of Queen Anne". Taking additional examples from the catalogue of medals, we find many others that are individually named: eg

"Medal commemorating death of Charles I"

"Medal commemorating the French invasion of Upper Germany"

"Medal commemorating the death of Maria Ludovica Beatrix (3rd wife of Francis II, Roman Emperor)"

"Medal commemorating Frederick William IV of Prussia in his role as sponsor at the christening of the Prince of Wales"

"Prize-medal for music"

In the foregoing examples the name given to the medal is created by reference to its purpose and the event with which it was associated. For the other objects (Examples 15, 16, 18) the individuality of the item is revealed only when the object-name is read in conjunction with its description, eg "floor-tile (decorated with) shield, a lion rampant reversed". The point at issue is to show that there is opportunity for variation in treatment within a structured record though, of course, such variation can be prohibited if desired by establishing suitable conventions to be followed by cataloguers. That variability or its prohibition is a matter of choice. The examples discussed here show that, whichever treatment of names is adopted, the structured record (if well devised) provides the opportunity to identify the object either as as a member of a group ('medals', 'floor-tiles', etc) or as a precise species (eg "prize-medal for music"), or even as a unique individual, eg "prize-medal for music awarded to ...."

A final example from the series of medals illustrates the potential for expansion of the structured record by inserting additional elements. As illustration, we take the full text of the record of the prize-medal:

Example 19   Prize medal for music

                    German

                    Unsigned

                    Bronze

        Obverse: DURCH POLYHYMNIENS MUND SICH DIE SEELE DIR KUND

                    Polyhymnia flying left, playing lyre.

        Reverse: Wreath of flowers and fruit.

        Centre vacant for inscription of recipient's name.

Here the usual elements found in all medal records are supplemented by description of the appearance of both sides of the medal, including reference to the inscriptions or legend and to imagery decorating its surfaces. This raises the question of whether comparable information on similar attributes could be provided in the records for other medals which are presently not described in such detail. Having considered this possibility, it is a natural consequence to suggest that a standard list of elements should be compiled to accommodate the fullest possible expression of a record. In the case of incomplete records, elements not represented by actual data could accept entries, eg 'none', 'not known', 'not applicable', which are more informative than their total omission.

In the experience of one major museum serving a conurbation of over a million people, it was found that many years elapsed after the initial introduction of structured records before the attempt was made to establish a standard list of information elements, even within a single catalogue. This stage was preceded by a period of 15-20 years during which gradual minor adjustments were made to the structure, classification and format of catalogue entries as a means of improving the utility of the records. Unfortunately, as is often the case, the changes were not co-ordinated but took place independently in several departments of the museum at the instigation of their respective curators. This resulted in the existence of a wide variety of record styles incorporating variant structures, formats, conventions and classifications.

EVOLUTION OF STRUCTURE

It is difficult to realise today how tentative were the first approaches to the writing of records in structured form: it seemed a radical departure from previous practice at a time when narrative text was the generally accepted style of recording. In the wake of a museum tradition that had served institutions for between 70 and 100 years, structuring was rather like putting the surgeon's knife into unskilled hands: it was an effective instrument but its cuts were, at first, too deep and not always in the right places. Some idea of the course of development of structure can be obtained by studying records produced in a single department of Fine Art over a period of ten years from the inception of the technique.

Example 20   PAUL NASH
                    Landscape of the Moon's First Quarter.
                    Oil on canvas: 24½ x 29½ ins.
                    Signed: Paul Nash
                    Insurance: £ x00
                    Purchased by the Corporation.

This was the kind of catalogue entry that replaced the discursive textual paragraph typical of earlier records. By contrast it is startling in its brevity and yet there is a familiarity about it. Both content and format are exactly as they were traditionally applied in the production of gallery labels for works of art. In fact this is not so much an innovation as an adaptation of existing method to a new purpose. The underlying intention was presumably to place limits on the length of the register entry to make it a more practical and utilitarian reference for administrative purposes. By so doing the inventory of works in the fine art collections took on a more organised appearance and the clear formatting made possible by the structured technique added greatly to the ease and convenience of consulting the records.

By its prominent position and the use of upper case characters, the artist's name was judged to be of paramount importance. The title of the work is stated as on an exhibition label, followed by the medium (oil/watercolour/pencil) and its 'support' (canvas/paper/etc), together with the dimensions of the picture. The authentication of the work is featured by stating the nature of the signature, an attribute that is peculiarly significant to a work of creative origin but one that has more extensive application. The record concludes with a statement on how the item was acquired and acknowledgement of the source from which it was obtained. The only element included which would not be seen on an exhibition label is the insured value. This picture is not classified in any sense but classificatory terms were among the first modifications to be introduced in later forms of record.

Within two years of adopting the first structured form, the museum changed both the structure and the format of its Fine Art records and at the same time introduced an element of classification. The new style is illustrated by the record for a Whistler print (below), of which the metaphor of "the surgeon's knife in unskilled hands" rings true.

Example 21   Prints
                  1945
                  Keen bequest
                  £xx.00
                  J. M. Whistler
                  The Forge
                  Whistler 1866
                  Etching: $7\frac{1}{2}$ x $12\frac{1}{2}$ ins.

41

The elements of this record are pared to the minimum and divested of all trace of headings and verbs, leaving the reader to guess at their precise significance. The record begins with the name of the class, ie 'Prints', to which the picture has been admitted and this is followed by the date (as year only) in which the work was received by the gallery. The source of its acquisition and the method of its acceptance are then summarised curtly in the phrase "Keen bequest", which evidently had adequate meaning for the curator at that time but, thirty years on, it gives little more than a clue to be pursued in the search for fuller information. The stated monetary value might be the price paid (if it had been purchased) but is in fact its insurance value. Then come the artist's name (relegated from its former prominence) and the title of the picture. The cryptic statement of the next element, "Whistler 1866", actually denotes how the print is signed and dated. This can be elusive in some other examples by Whistler where we find "Butterfly 1890" (the butterfly was a motif often used by this artist in place of a signature). Last of the data to be stated are the dimensions of the work and the technique by which the print was produced.

Example 22   Paintings - oils
July, 1962
Purchased from le Centre d'Art Contemporain, Berne, with the assistance of a x0% grant from the Victoria & Albert Museum.
Insurance value £x00
DERAIN, Andre (1880-1954)
Landscape near Cagnes
Signed on back: A.Derain
Oil on canvas: 25½ x 32 inches.

Despite the different appearance of this record compared with the last, the structure remains unchanged but the information within it is treated more expansively, as if to remedy the defects caused by the brevity of the preceding version. The date of its acceptance by the museum is expanded to include month as well as year. The acquisition statement is expressed as narrative, including all the necessary particulars of

42

method and circumstances in which it was acquired. The artist's name, distinguished in upper case, is augmented by his life-dates. The authentication is indicated by the phrase "signed on (the) back ...".

In this context the importance of conventions deserves remark. Paintings are usually said to be either 'signed' or 'not signed', but in the case of prints the operative word is more variable (eg 'signed' or 'inscribed'). A case in point is reported as "inscribed on the plate and in the margin ..." (personal names follow) but, due to the absence of a convention controlling the construction of the phrase, in some records we read only "on the plate J Green" or "in border P Emerson". This is somewhat cryptic without the operative verb 'signed' (or 'inscribed'). Incidentally, it would entirely defeat a computerised system depending on free-text search for word recognition, because the keywords are missing. Lack of conventions leads to variation in treatment between records which ought to be comparable and this causes ambiguity in interpretation.

A defect in the structure up to this point is the absence of class-ification of the subject, except at the most general level, eg 'Paintings/oils'. Although the subject of this record is obviously a landscape by virtue of its explicit title, on the other hand, immediate recognition of certain works as portraits is not assisted by the lack of reference to that term. Unless the format of the record is well understood and its (unstated) headings are known, it can even be difficult to distinguish the artist's name from that of the sitter!

Example 23 Sculpture - bronze
      Zoffoli, Giacomo (c1731-1785)
      Marcus Aurelius
      G.Z.F on side of saddle
      Bronze and marble
      First cast in 1763
      Bronze: height 40.2cm; width 22.3cm; diameter 34.2cm
      Overall: length 62.7cm; width 22.3cm; diameter 36.3cm
      White marble base. Bronze figure of Marcus Aurelius
      in short tunic, right hand outstretched, mounted on

horse with front hoof raised. A reduction of the classical group on the Capitol, Rome. The base follows that of the full-sized group designed by Michelangelo.

Other signed versions are known in:

1) Schloss Wilhelms-Hohe, near Kassel
2) Grune Gewolbe, Dresden; signed Giao. Zofoi F.1764
3) Saltram Park, Devon; signed G. Zoffoli F.

Literature: Hugh Honour, "Bronze Statuettes by Giacomo and Giovanni Zoffoli", Connoisseur CXLVIII pp 198-205. Purchased in May 1971 from David Peel & Co. Ltd. 2, Carlos Place, Mount Street, London;

with grant aid from the Victoria and Albert Museum. The structure of the record describing this sculpture clearly developed beyond the rather meagre report of Example 22. There is extra information on measurement that has its counterpart with reference to pictorial works in the dimensions of the support and of visible area masked by the mount: here the dimensions given distinguish the size of the bronze cast from that of the whole statue inclusive of its mounting (marble base). The final paragraph (above), refers to other casts which are replicas of the same work, ie it reports the existence of Facsimiles. The phenomenon applies in a corresponding manner to paintings which have been the subject of reproduction as prints: these too can be treated as a form of Facsimile. Two new elements of information, not restricted to sculpture, are a rather concise description of the subject and remarks relating to the Derivation of the work from its classical precedent. This is an instructive coincidence because in a single record we can perceive that a work of art may have replicas (copies) derived from it (each a 'facsimile') and yet can itself be derived, if it is modelled upon an earlier work ('precursor').

Example 24   Prints

Woodcut

Beham, Hans Sebald (1500-1550)

The Women's Bath

Signed in monogram H.S.B.

After 1525, before 1550

Circular, 11½ inches in diameter

Presented by the National Art Collections Fund, under provisions of the Thomas Ralston bequest.   April, 1968.

Insurance value: £x0

Printed border of leaf and baluster decoration.

Nine old and young female figures (some seated on benches, two standing) talking, washing feet or hair. Male figure on right holding an oil lamp.   Children, water tubs, combs, sponges and brushes in foreground.

Further notes: from the Bretano-Birckenstock Collection.

The classification here is elaborated into a two-tier scheme, the class named Prints having a sub-class Woodcuts. A change of format has repositioned the artist's name, together with the title of the picture (cf Example 22). A new element is introduced for the country of origin of the work. At this stage in the development of documentation there was no comprehensive structure into which information of every kind could be inserted. The appearance of adventitious information in the shape of 'Further notes' confirms that its occurrence was not foreseen.

Having examined a range of documentation in which information is expressed rather concisely, it becomes obvious that without headings or titles for the various fragments of information, the proper significance of the data may be missed. For use on an index card the names of headings would normally be pre-printed and if entered into a register (as these examples were) then the pages similarly should be pre-printed as forms for subsequent binding or as loose-leaf insertions.

The use of forms for recording information has its critics among curators (as witnessed by the remark, "I can put together an entry using far less paper") because, of course, on forms space is allocated for information that may not be available or even applicable. It also suffers from the drawback that writing space has to be partitioned between data categories and in each of them the space for entering data is limited. It is worth knowing that this awkward constraint is actually removed by some (but not all) of the computerised systems that are available for information management (cf Chapter 12).

STRUCTURING A TEXTUAL RECORD

In the development of structured records by a process of gradual refinement, there comes a point at which the fundamental attributes are regularly recognised and reported but there remains a body of variable information which seems less amenable to structuring. However, by reviewing many records of this kind it is possible to detect recurrent elements. In the next example, which is partially structured (its first 9 lines), we examine in detail the information held in the lengthy final paragraph with the aim of recognising further elements that could become part of a standard structure.

Example 25   Spode Plate
        Transfer printed earthenware
        England, Stoke-on-Trent
        c 1806 onwards
        Diameter 10 inches
        SPODE 54 impressed
        Purchased from J. I. Richards, per Messrs. Weller & Dufty,
        November 1969
        £3   10s.

Eight indents around the edge of plate, the border with blue transfer printed underglaze decoration of scrolls, conventional flowers and leaves, fleur-de-lys, the transfer join showing at the centre bottom. In the centre an imaginary scene with fabulous picturesque ruins: a gateway, two towers, a bridge, viaduct, with trees, a river, a figure with three cows, two figures with sheep, two swans on the river; known as the "Castle" pattern or by Hayden as "Tower".
cf. W L Little "Staffordshire Blue" plate 60, Dish Strainer marked Spode 13 and Spode D. also p.97 for dating "Castle" c 1805. cf. Arthur Hayden "Spode and his Successors" p.69 and pl. opposite p.70 for three pieces of "Tower" pattern. Sydney B Williams "Antique Blue and White Spode" on p.14 quotes L Jewitt "The Ceramic Art of Great Britain" 1883. Jewitt dates "Castle" pattern to 1806. Williams p.16 says

prototype engraving dated 1796-98. See also Williams p.120-2
and figs. 60-61 p.133. "Castle" derives from an aquatint
"The Gate of Sebastian" published J. Merigot 1st March 1796
and another of the "Ponte Molle" published 1st August 1796.
The Gate is the Porta Capena through which the Appian Way
passed. The arch is that of Drusus. The Ponte Molle was
built by Paulus Emilius, later Paulus Milvius. The tower was
raised by Belisarius and rebuilt by Pope Nicolas V.
E. Morton Nance 1942 "Pottery and Porcelain of Swansea and
Nantgarw" discusses the Swansea Bevington Co. variation of
'Castle'. It was also made by Barker, Bevans & Irwins; and
Clews Warranted Staffordshire. cf. Leonard Whiter "Spode"
1970 plate III, p.168 and fig.67 on p.169."

A paragraph of description forms the first section of text following the
concisely structured elements. This paragraph is composite because it
includes a description of the form of the plate, "eight indents around
the edge", and the method of surface decoration, "transfer printed
underglaze", the name given to the pattern ("known as the Castle ...
or Tower pattern") and also a descriptive list of its pictorial features.
These will be analysed more particularly in a subsequent discussion
(Chapter 8).

The remaining lengthy section of text appears to be an essay upon
the sources, both literary and otherwise, of the pictorial elements of
the pattern with references to the variations on this design produced
by other manufacturers. At first sight it appears intractable but,
noting the repetitive occurrence of citations of published work, it is
seen that the prose can be broken into several segments, each of them
referring to a single publication. This stage in the analysis is shown
in the annotated version of the record (below) in which authors' names
are underlined.

Example 25 (a):   Insertion of Headings.

DESCRIPTION/ Eight indents around edge of plate, the border with
blue transfer printed underglaze decoration of scrolls, conventional
flowers and leaves, fleur-de-lys, the transfer join showing at the

centre bottom. IMAGERY/ In the centre an imaginary scene with fabulous picturesque ruins: a gateway, two towers, bridge, ...etc known as the "Castle" pattern or by Hayden as "Tower".

1st CITATION/ W L Little "Staffordshire Blue" plate 60, Dish Strainer marked Spode 13 and Spode D; also p.97 dating "Castle" c1805. 2nd CITATION/ Arthur Hayden "Spode and his Successors" p.69 and pl. opposite p.70, three pieces of "Tower" pattern. 3rd CITATION/ Sydney B Williams "Antique Blue and White Spode" on p.14 quotes L Jewett /4th CITATION/ "The Ceramic Art of Great Britain" 1883. Jewitt dates "Castle" pattern to 1806.

Williams p.16 says prototype engraving dated 1796-98. See also Williams p.120-2 and figs. 60-61 p.133.

DERIVATION/ "Castle" derives from an aquatint "The Gate of Sebastian" published by J. Merigot 1st March 1796 and another of the "Ponte Molle" published 1st August 1796. The Gate is the Porta Capena through which passed the Appian Way. The arch is that of Drusus. The Ponte Molle was built by Paulus Emilius later changed to Milvius. The tower was raised by Belisarius and rebuilt by Pope Nicolas V. 5th CITATION/ E. Morton Nance "Pottery and Porcelain of Swansea and Nantgarw" 1942 discusses the Swansea Bevington & Co. variation of 'Castle'. It was also made by Barker, Bevans & Irwins; and Clews Warranted Staffordshire. 6th CITATION/ Leonard Whiter "Spode" 1970 plate III, p.168 and fig.67 on p.169.

The concluding stage in creating a structured record from an original narrative version is achieved by re-arranging the statements in order and presenting them in improved format. The terms underlined in the following revision of this record are inserted during editing.

Example 25 (b) The structured version.

DESCRIPTION Eight indents around the edge of plate, the border with blue [OMIT "transfer printed"; this being PROCESS] underglaze decoration of scrolls, conventional flowers and leaves, fleur-de-lys, the transfer join showing at the centre bottom.

48

IMAGERY	In the centre an imaginary 'landscape' (scene), includes fabulous picturesque ruins: gateway, two towers, bridge, ... etc; known as the Castle pattern or Tower pattern.
DERIVATION	The Castle pattern derives from an aquatint "The Gate of Sebastian" published by J. Merigot .... etc.
CITATION 1	W.L.Little "Staffordshire Blue" [INSERT date] pl.60 Dish marked Spode 13 and Strainer, Spode D, 'illustrated'. Castle pattern 'dated' c 1805 p.97.
CITATION 2	Arthur Hayden "Spode and his Successors" [INSERT date] opposite p.70 three pieces of Tower pattern 'illustrated' cf also p.69.
CITATION 3	Sydney B. Williams "Antique Blue and White Spode" [INSERT date] p.16, says prototype engraving is dated 1796-98. cf also p.1202 and figs.6061 p.133 'illustrated'.
CITATION 4	L.Jewitt "The Ceramic Art of Great Britain" (1883) Castle pattern 'dated' to 1806 (cited by S.B.Williams).
CITATION 5	E. Morton Nance "Pottery and Porcelain of Swansea and Nantgarw" (1942) discusses the Swansea Bevington Co. variation of Castle pattern. It was also made by Barker, Bevans & Irwins; and Clews Warranted Staffordshire.
CITATION 6	Leonard Whiter "Spode" (1970) pl.3 p.168 and fig.67 on p.169 'illustrated'.

The gradual development and continual refinement of structure in the evolution of records can be detected by studying catalogues in museums in which the actual documentation has not been revised since the entries were written. The following example represents a more advanced stage in structuring, displaying an increased number of defined elements in comparison with records already discussed. It concludes with a paragraph of text which is not differentiated into elements, though it is a simple matter to convert this into structured form, beginning with the statement describing the Imagery. To assist immediate interpretation and their recognition in later discussion, the elements are named in the margin. Some of these will be formally recognised as components in a new structural framework to be described in Chapter 6 and following.

Example 26

Classification]	Ceramics / Enamel / Plaque
Maker's Name]	Gertrude May Hart, afterwards Partridge
Maker's Role]	Designer and maker
Maker's Life Dates]	1881-1917
Materials]	Enamel on copper
Process used]	Translucent and semi-translucent basse taille
Where made]	Birmingham, England
Date made]	1906 (probably)
Size]	Sight: 4.5 x 7.0 cm
"]	Frame: 13.75 x 16.50 cm
Maker's Mark]	small gold hart in lower R corner
Presented by]	Miss Joan Partridge
Presented as]	Gift
Donor's address]	49 Meadbeck Avenue, Kenton, Middlesex
Valuation]	£x0.00
Imagery]	Bust of mediaeval lady in profile dressed in robe of brown and purple, with jewelled head-dress, against red background. //
Description]	Dark brown frame with small green square inset. //
Inscription]	On the back there is a description of the plaque as a design in colours //
Derivation]	from a reproduction of Da Vinci's portrait of Beatrice D'Este, //
Maker's Mark]	signature Hart //and some obliterated writing.

Reviewing these points, there is a classification in three parts but it is a mixed classification: the major class and sub-class being descriptors by material and only one part defining the type of object ('plaque'). Materials used in its creation are stated again (5th line), repeating the term 'enamel', but no mention is made of the materials in the frame. The technique employed in its fabrication is mentioned by reference to 'basse taille'. Two sets of measurements are given, one of the frame and the other (called 'sight') defining the visible area of the image.

The artist's signature (Maker's Mark) is reported to be present on the back of the object but in what medium is not stated: is it engraved on the copper or painted, or is it pencilled onto a back panel forming part of the frame? Also on the back, there is mentioned a description of the design which clearly is a statement of derivation but again no indication is given of the form of this label. The description of the image itself can be separated from that of the frame. The artist's name is given in two forms, maiden name and married name and the artist's role is specified in two terms ('designer' and 'maker') to show that she was both the originator of the design as a visual concept and also the technician or craftsperson who executed the enamelling process.

In many ways, therefore, this catalogue record approximates in its details to the elements that would be expected in a modern structured description. What is needed to stabilize the process of cataloguing is recognition of the individual components as named elements within a framework which can be applied routinely to assist cataloguers in their work. It would be a great advantage if such a framework possessed the property of plasticity to enable it to be moulded to the information needs of curators concerned with collections of every kind. The Museum Documentation Association, Cambridge, England, has for almost a decade endeavoured to promote such a concept but the formalised style in which it presents its standards (and to some extent its terminology also) unfortunately obscures the underlying philosophy. Insistence upon the observance of prescribed conventions concentrates the readers' attention on the mechanics of documentation and, besides giving an impression of rigidity, disguises the ultimate aims of the whole scheme.

In contrast to this, the framework which is introduced here in the following chapters is presented as a logical construction of concepts already familiar to curators, which is designed to be flexible in many different cataloguing situations and to serve as a vehicle for the essentially practical requirements of managing collections.

Chapter 4

Choosing the vocabulary

WHAT IS TECHNICAL DESCRIPTION?

No matter whether records are written as narrative free-text or as highly segmented data, the choice of words is of paramount importance. In everyday speech and writing we tend to exercise our freedom of vocabulary to greater or lesser degree and we "ring the changes" by using variable expressions and synonyms for items, actions and events. In cataloguing, such wanton application of words is not permissible: the only virtue is constancy. It is the cataloguer's fundamental task to find words that are apt in every context and to apply them with single-minded consistency. There is no other skill so indispensible to cataloguing as the disciplined use of language. If a strict vocabulary is one contribution to achieving this, then precision in applying it is the other essential factor.

A good description of a museum object is one that succeeds in combining an account of the attributes of the individual item with a synopsis of the features which it shares with comparable objects. Paradoxically, describing particular features of detail is probably easier than describing the whole object. The vocabulary applicable to detailed aspects of an object is often comprised of specific terms which are, by definition, less likely to be applied in different contexts and with other meanings. However, in the extreme case specific terms are technical terms, that is, members of a language within-a-language. Technical terms are words of restricted usage which are, therefore, readily known and understood mainly by specialists in the subject to which they are applied. Obviously there are occasions when technical terms are unavoidable but their use should be tempered with common sense so as not to exclude readers of the catalogue who do not claim expertise within a narrow discipline.

Example 27   Pair of gilt-bronze wall sconces.

     Each comprises three richly foliated branches terminating in inturned eagles' heads, which carry a small baluster below a socket ornamented with foliage and fruit, each with a simple drip-pan with a knurled edge. Its wall-mounted shaft is in two parts, the upper comprising a fluted vase from which rises a thyrsus entwined with laurel; its lower part consisting of a Satyr's mask above a trophy of pan-pipes and cymbals entwined with ivy and suspended by tasselled ribbons: having a pendant swag of flowers and fruit below the branches.

In the above paragraph, the words underlined are terms that might cause the reader to pause and possibly to reach for a dictionary. When reading this description we encounter some uncertainties in our under-standing, because these words are not generally used in everyday language or, if so, they are used in quite different circumstances and convey meanings that are not relevant in this record. Such terms are features of a technical description. They may be of assistance to anyone who understands their special meanings but for the uninitiated their presence obstructs our comprehension.

    It may be argued that the above description is succinct and would be readily understood with the object in hand, when its aptness would be apparent, but the point is that the description must serve in lieu of inspection and a visual appreciation of the appearance of this object depends entirely on the implication of those words. Despite its refer-ence to a feature of plant life, 'foliated' is not in use as a botanical term and its meaning in the above example differs totally from the connotation it would have if describing a rock specimen (it is applied in geology as a technical term). A 'trophy', in common usage, applies to an object of almost any kind that is acquired as a prize.

There is no escaping the convenience of a specialised vocabulary within each discipline: every sphere of collecting has its own terminology and this becomes familiar with apprenticeship and participation. However, when special terminology is adopted for catalogue use, it should be for reasons of exactness and only when no commoner term can be substituted without ambiguity. Never should special terms be used as a form of secret language to shroud information in obscurity: the purpose of cataloguing is, above all, to make knowledge more widely available. Particularly in the cataloguing of public collections, it is preferable to use a non-specialised vocabulary as far as this is compatible with accuracy and to keep to a minimum the use of special terms.

Considering the extreme variety of objects and materials contained in a major multi-disciplinary museum, in terms of documentation there can be no doubt that the total vocabulary that might be employed for recording is encyclopaedic. It is tempting for a curator to emphasise that tendency by using narrow specialised vocabularies within distinct disciplines but this would have the unfortunate effect of restricting information to persons who are already knowledgeable. Being aware of the requirements and interests of a wider audience, curators can ensure that the records they write are intelligible without specialist knowledge.

The following examples illustrate the point and raise a question. How knowledgeable do you have to be to interpret them completely? Ask yourself whether you too need a dictionary to interpret these records.
(a) Axe-head "found by donor about 1930 during soil-stripping about one foot deep in stony aggregate at clay-pit off Newbury Lane".
(b) Seal-matrix "silver, mounted in ebony, assayed at Chester 1906 (bearing) achievement of arms and inscription ...".
(c) Japanese Sword. "Curved steel blade, copper habaki, wooden hilt covered with fish-skin and partially wrapped in cloth.
The words underlined in these examples are used as descriptors of materials, parts of an object, or constructions, etc. All of them can be regarded as technical terms which tend to obscure the information for

the non-specialist reader. None of them is indispensible and alternative expressions could quite simply be substituted. Adjectival terms of questionable value are even more frequently encountered (d - f) and could be deleted without detriment to the description or in each case an adjective from the general vocabulary could be substituted, eg,

(d) "approximately half of a leaf-shaped dagger of infacially worked translucent flint";

(e) "bowl of colour-coated ware with curved rim and barbotine decoration of leaves";

(f) "finely inscribed figure of seated dog, facing left, above single line of demotic inscription which reads ...".

CONTROLLED VOCABULARY

There are many arguments for restricting the range of vocabulary to something less than a literary competition might demand. It is an axiom that museum records must be comprehensible, not only to the writer of a particular record but to a wide readership which includes museum professionals in other disciplines, administrators, auditors and an enquiring public clientele.

Having established this, we can now examine the proposition that more stringent self-discipline is needed in the use of words. The next step is to reduce or eliminate the gratuitous use of synonyms so that a preferred term emerges. The aim will be to apply this preferred term consistently to objects, features or attributes, as the case may be, for the sake of clarity and to emphasise comparability between the items described. Even when it is necessary to emphasise a difference, this practice serves us well because we know that the use of a different word is intentional and that it discriminates objects that might otherwise be confused.

The idea of introducing controlled vocabulary immediately focusses thought on the proper definition of terms and for this reason it is to be strongly recommended. It is especially important for nouns which are used to designate objects, their construction, their composition, parts, origins and usage, etc. Control of vocabulary will ensure, for example, that 'drawing' and 'illustration' are never confused, the former being a designation of the two-dimensional image produced by certain techniques while the latter designates the intention of the graphic artist when the resulting image is a faithful representation of a subject. For example, "the drawing, in charcoal on buff paper, is a topographic illustration of Canterbury Cathedral". In adopting the word 'drawing' as the preferred term for the object, it is essential to define it, eg by stating that it is to be used for all graphic works produced by hand in any of the following media: charcoal, chalk, pastel, crayon, pencil, ink, etc. With such a definition in use, one can be reasonably confident that a degree of consistency has been introduced which would otherwise be lacking and that catalogue entries will be more meaningful as a result.

A controlled vocabulary carries the implication that certain words are approved and therefore are to be regarded as permitted terms, while other near-equivalent words are not approved and are therefore not permitted to appear in catalogue records: they must be replaced by substituting the corresponding permitted term. The reasons for this seemingly pedantic exercise will become abundantly clear from inspection of some simple illustrations, as follow.

In the collections of many local museums of social history, there are plentiful examples of substitute coins manufactured in base metals and often these are stamped with a trader's name to serve as tokens, (proof of payment accepted), for use in purchasing goods or services. They are variously known as 'tokens', 'tickets', 'checks' or 'counters'. These four terms are synonyms referring to the same class of objects but to use all of them indiscriminately is unhelpful because it suggests either that we do not distinguish between them or, more importantly, that there is significance in the choice of word which in reality does not exist. Here then is an obvious case for selecting a 'permitted term' and using this term to the exclusion of the other three.

We have already referred to 'drawing' and 'illustration' with an attempt to distinguish them. However these are not the only possible terms that may be found in records relating to drawn images. The word 'sketch' has been applied to illustrative representations of scenes as well as to preliminary versions of more permanent works, and in the last sense the word 'cartoon' is also a synonym (quite apart from its popular meaning). By invoking controlled vocabulary we can ensure that only one meaning attaches to our use of a permitted term. Without a controlled vocabulary, a word could be applied rather loosely to describe an item for which a better term exists.

The concept of controlled vocabulary is seen most clearly where it is not complicated by differences in definition of the words undergoing selection. If alternative descriptors have directly comparable meanings then the case for selecting one of them and rejecting use of the others is obvious. It is particularly of advantage when records are searched to retrieve those filed under a certain term: the enquirer may not think of all the possible synonyms and in any case it is laborious to repeat searches of the index merely to ensure that all relevant records have been found. This is as true for computerised record retrieval as it is for manual searching of card indexes: computer-aided systems will not perform any miracles if the vocabulary of catalogue entries is defective.

SELECTING PERMITTED TERMS
The criteria needed to select suitable terms for cataloguing and to recognise and reject terms that are unsuitable for this purpose have been derived from the characteristics of words that succeed in practice and by learning from mistakes. Among the foremost characteristics of good catalogue terms is freedom from ambiguity: words that have only a single meaning are preferable to those that have different inferences depending on context. However, if a word does apply in more than one situation, it is important that its meanings are quite separate in their implications so that confusion can be avoided when interpreting records. The word 'sketch', for example, does not meet this criterion as its various meanings are closely allied and the broad manner in which this general-purpose term is applied allows shades of meaning to grade imperceptibly from one to another. In the interests of comprehension it is also important that, for use as a catalogue term, the word should be widely known and that it should be applied in the sense most commonly understood. There is a serious risk of misinterpretation by the reader if a well-known word is not used in its ordinary sense but in a special sense, either derived from a dictionary or contrived by the curator.

57

'Cartoon', for example, may mean quite different things to a curator of fine art, to a film archivist, to a journalist and to a layman (whose interpretation may vary according to his erudition). The effective qualities of terms being considered for cataloguing can be evaluated by testing them individually against the following algorithm, which applies these criteria.

ALGORITHM FOR SELECTION OF PERMITTED TERMS

1> state the WORD

2> DEFINE its meaning

3> Does it have ALTERNATIVE meanings? --->

      NO ---> see Point 31

      YES --> see Point 4

    31> Is this word widely KNOWN? --->

         NO ---> Place at END of RESERVE LIST. see Point 7

         YES --> see Point 9

4> Are its other meanings DISTINCT? --->

      NO, liable to misinterpretation /ambiguity ---> see Point 41

      YES --> see Point 5

    41> Reject this word. see Point 7

5> Does MUSEUM CONTEXT exclude irrelevant meanings? --->

      NO ---> see Point 51

      YES --> see Point 6

    51> Place this word at END of RESERVE LIST; see Point 7

6> Place this word at TOP of RESERVE LIST;   see Point 7

7> Choose another word of SIMILAR MEANING   --->

      If new word FOUND ---> return to Point 1

      If new word not available ---> see Point 8

8> Take TOP word from RESERVE LIST --->

    81> Is its COMMON meaning RELEVANT? (to museum applications)

         NO ---> Reject this term.   Return to Point 8

         YES --> see Point 9

9> ADOPT this word as a PERMITTED TERM.   Return to Point 7

The following example illustrates the use of the algorithm as an aid in compiling a controlled vocabulary, taking the selection procedure step by step and using words that have already been discussed as options: firstly, the numismatic examples. Consideration of each word is marked by an alphabetic reference in the left margin, thus lines marked 'A' examine the term 'token', 'B' repeats the process for 'ticket' and so on. Numbered references to 'Point' relate each line to the equivalent point in the Algorithm. Asterisks denote definitions according to the "Shorter Oxford Dictionary".

A   Point 1: the word is 'token'

A   Point 2: it means: "a disc or other item received in proof of payment that can be exchanged for goods or service" *

A   Point 3: other meaning: "a sign of favour" *

A   Point 4: Yes, this meaning is totally distinct.

A   Point 5: In museum context, the second meaning (Point 3) is excluded, being irrelevant

A   Point 6: 'token' is placed at the top of our reserve list of terms

      Point 7: we choose an alternative term

B   Point 1: the word is 'ticket'

B   Point 2: it means: "proof of payment, usually in form of paper or card, for a service initiated at time of purchase" *

B   Point 3: other meanings? None.

B   Point 31: the word 'ticket' is widely known

B   Point 9: 'ticket' (defined in B/2) adopted as PERMITTED TERM

      Point 7: we choose another possible term

C   Point 1: the word is 'check'

C   Point 2: it means: "proof of payment, as with a counterfoil" *

C   Point 3: other meanings: "proof of thing done, action taken, often in the form of a tally" *

C   Point 4: these meanings are not distinct and could be confused

C   Point 41: 'check' is rejected and scheduled as an INVALID TERM

      Point 7: we choose another word

D   Point 1: the word is 'counter'

D   Point 2: it means: "a form of currency in limited circulation" *

D	Point 3:	other meaning: "instrument for counting, making a tally"*
D	Point 4:	these meanings are not distinct and could cause misinterpretation
D	Point 41:	'counter' is rejected: scheduled as an INVALID TERM
D	Point 7:	we do not find another possible term and turn to the Reserve List
D	Point 8:	the first (and only) word on the list is 'token'
D	Point 81	its common meaning is perfectly relevant
D	Point 9:	'token' (defined in A/2) adopted as PERMITTED TERM

Resulting from this analysis, we have selected just two permitted terms ('ticket' and 'token') which according to accepted definitions possess distinct meanings, and both words should be used henceforth in cataloguing) with strict observance of these definitions. We have found that two other terms, 'check' and 'counter', do not pass the selection test and these are now regarded as invalid terms which henceforth will not be permitted for any definitive use in cataloguing. The same procedure can be followed using the terms discussed for graphic art:

E	Point 1:	the word is 'drawing'
E	Point 2:	meaning: "image created by use of a pencil, pen or solid medium to apply pigment" *
E	Point 3:	other meanings? None.
E	Point 31:	the word 'drawing' is widely known
E	Point 9:	'drawing' (defined in E/2) adopted as PERMITTED TERM
	Point 7:	we choose another possible term
F	Point 1:	the word is 'illustration'
F	Point 2:	meaning: "an image that is a faithful representation of an object" *
F	Point 3:	other meanings: "graphic representation of a fictional scene or event" *
F	Point 4:	these meanings are distinct and not liable to confusion in a museum context
F	Point 5:	both meanings are appropriate, neither is irrelevant

F	Point 6:	'illustration' is placed at TOP of RESERVE LIST
	Point 7:	we choose another word
G	Point 1:	the word is 'sketch'
G	Point 2:	meaning: "a drawing made on location, visual notes" *
G	Point 3:	other meanings: "preliminary drawing, preparatory work for a more studied composition" *
G	Point 4:	these meanings are not distinct in a museum context
G	Point 41:	'sketch' is rejected and scheduled as an INVALID TERM.
	Point 7:	we choose another word
H	Point 1:	the word is 'cartoon'
H	Point 2:	meaning: "drawing made as a design at the same size for a finished work in another medium" *
H	Point 3:	other meanings? "satirical or humorous drawing used as vehicle for comment" AND "humorous cinematic sequence created by animation" *
H	Point 4:	these meanings are distinct but depend on context for correct interpretation
H	Point 5:	the museum context does not exclude irrelevant meanings
H	Point 51:	the word 'cartoon' is placed at END of RESERVE LIST
H	Point 7:	no alternative word found
H	Point 8:	from reserve list the word 'cartoon' is reconsidered
H	Point 81:	its most COMMON meaning is not relevant to (art-) museum applications. 'cartoon' is rejected as INVALID.

If, for a moment, we assume that the word 'cartoon' is under review for use in cataloguing a film archive, using exactly the same procedure, we discover that the outcome can be quite different, as follows [J Point 2]. Cartoon is defined as "humorous cinematic sequence using animation".* The precise path of selection depends upon the answers provided at each step of the test but in this case it is likely that 'cartoon' will emerge as a permitted term whichever route is taken. At H Point 3, supposing the response is "No, no other meanings", then in answer to Point 31 the reply is "Yes, the word is widely known". This leads directly to Point 9 and the recommendation that 'cartoon' be adopted as a permitted term within the meaning defined at J Point 2. Alternatively, if the other possible meanings of this word are recognised at Point 3, then at Point 4 the answer must be "Yes, other meanings are distinct". In the context of a museum of photography the ensuing question, (J5) "Does the museum context exclude irrelevant meanings?" will ensure that the word is placed in the reserve list for further consideration and ultimately it will be accepted on the basis that its most commonly understood meaning is the relevant one for film.

By applying this algorithm as a test for the suitability of words in cataloguing, it is possible to build up a vocabulary of terms which are generally known, unambiguous and which are applied in a sense that is never obscure. Trial use of the method soon brings out the importance of careful thought over definitions, including both the primary definition expressing the sense in which the cataloguer wishes to apply the term and the definition of other possible meanings which the cataloguer is aware of.

For museums that fail to recognise the importance of controlled vocabulary the main consequence is the proliferation of variant semantic applications of common words. To put this plainly, the more versatile a word is, the more diverse and the less consistent its usage becomes. This has only to infiltrate a minority of records to have a detrimental effect on the entire catalogue: when uncontrolled usage is endemic then a catalogue dissolves into chaos.

EFFECTS ON RECORD RETRIEVAL
By allowing uncontrolled use of common terms to persist in records that were probably written many years ago, prospects for converting card files to computerised retrieval systems are seriously compromised. Further illustrations are hiding in every card catalogue and in almost every page of register. What can be the meaning of 'tunic' when the word is used in such a variety of ways? eg
    "Train Driver's tunic ...."
    "Afternoon Dress, high-necked bodice with tunic front"
    "Bronze Figure of Marcus Aurelius in short tunic ...."
Bear in mind that when a word-search is implemented by computer in the mode known as 'free-text search' (word-matching), the machine's

recognition of the term is absolute and infallible, provided that the required word exists in exactly the form stated. The resultant retrieval presents every incidence of that term regardless of its context, its usage or its sense. If it has been loosely or carelessly applied when the records were written, it may prove to be almost invalid as a term of significance (what is generally called a 'keyword'). A lexicon reduces duplication of terms by avoiding gratuitous use of synonyms: it controls the use of every term in accordance with a stated definition.

Textual records are inherently weak on classification because they are not a product of structured concepts: objects are merely named (often without controlled vocabulary) and in general simple names are not supplemented by classified names to indicate their membership of a group or class. In consequence, there is a proliferation of varietal names and a virtual absence of consistent terms. Advocates of free-text retrieval systems (especially computer software salespersons) often recommend their adoption for just such situations, on the assumption that if no uniformity of vocabulary existed at input, at least you can access data by whatever terms were used. In practice this may prove to be very inconvenient and at worst ineffective. Suppose we have to work with a mixed catalogue of a very large costume collection of which 60% of records are textual, 40% being partly structured and classified. The options for extracting records of any particular category using common group terms are extremely limited as in the following examples:

Example 28   Men's Costume: English Court Dress
> worn by an ancestor of the donor, Sir Montagu Trafford. Black silk Cocked Hat, with rosette. Black silk "Wig Bag". Coat single-breasted, blue with stand collar. 8 cut steel buttons on right front; 8 simulated button-holes on left. Plain cuffs with 3 similar buttons to each and pointed pocket flaps with one button below each point. 6 buttons behind; 2 at the waist, 2 at centre of the skirt and 2 at the hem. Breeches of the same material with 3 small steel buttons at the knees, buckles missing. For type see p.76 in:
> "Dress Worn at Court", Harrison's and Sons, Pall Mall (1912).

Example 29   Dress. Silk damask, separate bodice and skirt.
              Skirt, full for crinoline, with deep flounce.
              Bodice with deep pointed boned waist, edged with
              ribbon; triangular shoulder epaulettes with flared
              sleeves. Applied irregular rope silk design in
              military style; pearl buttons.
              English; c. 1866, worn by Elizabeth S Peel.

Example 30   Evening Dress
              Brocade and crepe; separate bodice and skirt.
              Skirt with inset panel of yellow crepe at the front,
              tapes attached inside to hold bustle. Bodice with
              pointed boned waist; yellow crepe inset front in the
              front, revers faced with blue satin.
              English; 1884 ?, worn by Mrs Winifred Davies;
              made by Poncerot & Langstaff, 25 Albert Place, Kensington.

All three of these records are infallibly retrieved by a search on the
keywords 'dress' and 'English' in response to a request for information
on women's dresses in the costume collection. Contrary to intent, one
of them describes male costume, which should be disqualified by the
keyword 'Men's'. Unfortunately, the exclusive term 'Women's' cannot be
specified because the textual records describing women's garments do
not contain that essential term. No alternative descriptors can be
found in these records for women's dresses that do not also occur in
entries for male costumes such as the Court Dress. Even the word
'skirt' occurs in describing the male coat.

When using free-text retrieval methods on documents that were not
designed and written with this method in mind, we can expect that some
spurious records will be selected in addition to those which are the
proper target of the search. On the other hand, if the opportunity
exists to write the records with the intention of employing free-text
retrieval methods, the incidence of rogue records (not conforming to
the target group) can be reduced. The single most important step
towards achieving satisfactory retrieval is to prepare records in accord-

ance with a conceptual structure: the need is for organised thinking in the process of creating the record. Almost equally important, every statement should include some keywords that match permitted terms in a lexicon. Statements may then be written in natural language, without need for codes or abbreviations (though these also have their place), providing that the computer software allows word-search to be targeted at any selected paragraph. Preferably it will also have a facility, later described in Chapter 12, to enable the enquirer to specify the length of phrase containing the search terms for retrieval. The inherent scarcity of classificatory terms in narrative statements needs to be remedied by attaching supplementary keywords, in effect comprising a Classification Statement (Chapter 8), and by exerting strict control over vocabulary.

COMPILING A LEXICON

A careful distinction should be made between schemes of classification and efforts to establish standard terminology: they often overlap but in essence they are entirely separate concepts. A new classification such as the Social History and Industrial Classification (SHIC 1983) inevitably involves innovative nomenclature but its essential role is to introduce a re-organisation of material and not necessarily to impose its vocabulary. However, widespread adoption of a classification is often a prelude to demand for a standard reference vocabulary (in natural sciences both phenomena are closely correlated). There has recently been noticed a general movement towards the creation of lexicons in most fields of museum interest. Many initiatives are taken in individual museums, for example the work of Chenhall (1978) whose "Nomenclature" became a model for others -- but problems of dissemination tend to limit their wider currency. Effective vocabularies of object names and other attributes have been developed independently in England by Hertford-shire Curators Group, the Wiltshire Museums Service (Norgate, 1987), the Museum of London (unpublished) and others, each for their local purposes. A recent survey in south-eastern England revealed that almost one hundred museums were using their own internal conventions on vocabulary (Holm, 1986). However, co-ordinating groups are already beginning to influence the construction of vocabulary and may sometime publish definitive reference lists. Notable among these are plans for a scientific and technological object thesaurus being developed by a committee of specialist curators in Britain and a more wide-ranging study by the Museum Terminology Working Party hosted by the MDA. The Museum Documentation Association itself is advocating acceptance of agreed terminology in connection with its recently produced data entry software for microcomputers, which it hopes will encourage curators to standardise their vocabularies.

A lexicon is a list of approved terms and because this is the means of ensuring control of vocabulary, it is an essential tool for cataloguers. It serves as a dictionary of terms that have been selected for use in museum records. A handbook should be produced in every cataloguing department to establish guidance on procedures, structural organisation of records, conventions, vocabulary, etc and a comprehensive lexicon forms an essential part of this. Both the handbook and the lexicon itself contain the precedents that must be followed by cataloguers and curators to ensure that the system of records is perpetuated and continually maintained to standards that have been well devised.

Every word included in the lexicon should be accompanied by a definition of the meaning attached to it by the institution for its own purposes. From all that has been said already in this chapter, it is axiomatic that the definitions approved in the lexicon have passed the scrutiny of comparative selection, eg by use of the algorithm, and that they relate closely to generally accepted usage. It is not enough to compile a lexicon by abstract thought, even with the aid of a standard dictionary: only by reference to real museum records can we examine the multifarious contexts in which particular words are sometimes used.

Progress can only be made on the basis of a substantial archive of records accumulated over a long period of years. This archive probably exists in most institutions housing collections as the result of earlier documentary methods. In the case of collections previously unrecorded, for which a suitable vocabulary must be initiated, curators need to seek the advice of others who have catalogued similar collections before drawing up a lexicon for themselves. The essential prerequisite is to examine in depth a large archive in which the aptness of terms used for naming, describing and classifying can be assessed. In the course of this process areas of ambiguity, inconsistency and other difficulties can be recognised and noted so that they may be avoided or corrected when selecting and defining permitted terms.

An additional function of controlled vocabulary is to exclude the use of obscure terms which may be unfamiliar for various reasons, eg colloquial names, localised in use, or terms from another language. Some obscure terms are allusions to precedent, eg 'barbotine', indicating resemblance to an already known item from whose name the term is derived. It is counter-productive to employ obscure terms: it actually hinders the reader's understanding of what the record purports to describe. The proper aim must be to compile a word-list or lexicon, using terms that are both apt and meaningful to the widest possible readership. This not only avoids the charge of elitism but also greatly facilitates the use of computers.

The force of these remarks may alarm some museum professionals who believe that anyone who has taken sufficient interest in his special field will be fully acquainted with the terms that are habitually used. No doubt this is true but the aspiring amateur collector and beginning student have a quite arduous task in assimilating a subject vocabulary which is littered with words whose only merit is that they are (or were once) fashionable. As stability of nomenclature is an underlying necessity in cataloguing, it is better to provide a core of description that does not depend on ephemeral terms and, if you must include them, to append such terms in footnotes to the record. They can comprise all names of styles, trends and traditions of localised or temporal fashion which do not have general currency and whose equivalence to approved terms can be defined in a thesaurus (Orna and Pettitt, 1980; Townley and Gee, 1980).

REFERENCES

Chenhall, R.G. (1978) "Nomenclature for museum cataloguing: a system
for classifying man-made objects" Nashville, Tenn.:
American Association for State and Local History. 512pp.

Holm, S. (1986) "Terminology Control" MDA Information vol.10 no.3 p37.

Hunter, E. and K.G.B. Bakewell (1983) "Cataloguing" 2nd edn.
London: Clive Bingley. New York: K.G. Saur. 222pp.

Norgate, M. (1987) "Wiltshire Museums Group Conventions"
Devizes: published by the author. Loose-leaf c. 470pp.
available from Museum Documentation Assoc., Cambridge.

Orna, E. and C.Pettitt (1980) "Information Handling in Museums"
London: Clive Bingley. New York: K.G. Saur. 190pp.

Roberts, D.A. (1986) editor "The State of Documentation in non-national
Museums in south-east England" Cambridge, England:
Museum Documentation Association. MDA Occasional
Paper No.9; 58pp.

SHIC Working Party (1983) "Social History and Industrial Clssification"
Sheffield, England: Centre for English Cultural Tradition
and Language.

Townley, H.M. and R.D.Gee (1980) "Thesaurus-making: grow your own
word-stock" London: Andre Deutsch 206pp.

Chapter 5

Conventions

Conventions are rules governing style, and in the context of cataloguing they include all those features affecting the presentation of data in legible form, both on paper and on a computer screen. Conventions should be constructive: their effect should be to ease the reading of information and make it mentally digestible. When conventions are introduced, the reader's comprehension of records should be improved both in speed and accuracy while the mechanisms that make it possible should be unobtrusive. Conventions operate by ensuring consistency in presenting comparable facts. If the factual statements concerning two distinct objects are intended to bear comparison, they should both appear in the same formal arrangement, using the same syntax, the same rules of punctuation and the same typographic effects. For example, if personal names and titles are treated in a consistent manner then possible ambiguities are avoided, such as confusing an unusual surname with a common forename (eg John Henry).

Among conventions in general use, abbreviations are frequently encountered but they are not always distinct from one another (unique) or consistent. In museum records, to be effective, abbreviations must be standardised so that data of quite distinct meaning can be expressed briefly yet without risk of confusion. Because conventions are accepted as part of our everyday use of language, they are absorbed into our mental machinery for interpreting written symbols. It is important, therefore, that the conventions which museums adopt for their own use do not conflict with those understood in ordinary communication. If common punctuation marks are accorded particular significance for the purposes of catalogues, the partitioning of information into its natural elements becomes more clearly apparent. On the other hand, if typographic characters (symbols) are used as marks of special significance unrelated to their ordinary connotation, the reader is forced to 'unlearn' the normal interpretation and in its place substitute an unfamiliar one. This is counter-productive. The use of variant typefaces (eg bold and italic) and controlled use of upper and lower case characters can enhance legibility and assist in differentiating elements of information, for example, in naming the titles of publications and pictures. Typographical devices of this kind are quickly assimilated by the reader and they strengthen the significance of the data thus presented.

Four aspects of documentary presentation are governed by conventions and all of them may be applied to museum records with benefit in greater or lesser degree. These are:

1. Abbreviations
2. Punctuation
3. Syntax
4. Typography.

Preferably, the conventions adopted should operate as a refinement of normal conventions using marks that do not seem unfamiliar in their context. It is not the aim of cataloguing to translate coherent language into a form of code that must be deciphered but to express particulars of information with the least ambiguity. Conventions must be directed to achieving that objective.

The extent to which new conventions are introduced beyond those in general currency is a matter of choice and few museums are found operating conventions that do not include some of their own making. Special conventions are at their lowest incidence in the old-fashioned narrative records written in standard prose using ordinary syntax and punctuation. However, textual records can include typographical effects such as changes of fount (italic, bold, capitals) and abbreviations.

Broadly speaking, the need for conventions increases when records are converted from purely textual to structured forms. The need for conventions is greatly reinforced when adopting computerised methods for handling records. Many conventions, especially of syntax (word-order) and the use of punctuation marks and typographic symbols can only be developed in relation to the particular data-handling methods to be employed. Conventions that are admirable when used on cards in manual systems may be ill-suited for use in computer systems. Indeed, among the latter there are such considerable differences between the manipulative processes of free-text retrieval systems and database management systems that appropriate conventions may differ correspondingly in these two situations.

SYNTAX CONVENTIONS

To emphasise what is considered to be important and to explain the relationship between parts of an object, its construction and decoration, narrative description employs long sentences with subordinate clauses and other constructions. This is not necessary in catalogue descriptions because the reader is mentally orientated and expects to find detailed information presented in an orderly series of particulars. The reader of a catalogue needs to be presented with the facts in a manner that is not complicated by elaborate forms of expression. By reducing the number of ancillary words, the clarity of factual information is greatly improved. The changes of syntax required to effect this involve removing active verbs, omitting both definite and indefinite article and reducing dependent clauses to a single adjective or phrase. In practice this is a great deal easier than it sounds. In Example (31) the words enclosed in square brackets can be omitted as being superfluous, while leaving the substance of the description unimpaired.

Example 31   "[The main] material [of the dress is] green with a rosebud pattern and black dots. [The] bodice [is] lined in calico [and stiffened] with whalebone.   [It] hooks [together] down the front [the fastening being] hidden by [an] inset of lace and chiffon with black velvet ribbon stripes.   [There is a] high lace collar [round the neck, sewn] with [a] fringe, [and a] broad flat lace [collar] on the shoulders continuing down the front as a ruffle. [The] leg-of-mutton sleeves [are] narrow [at the] wrist [where they are trimmed] with a fringe [and have a series of] tucks on the upper arm."

To demonstrate further the syntax conventions recommended, in the next example a description is taken from a record which already shows a simplified construction and notable economy of expression (comparable with the product of editing in the previous example).

Example 32   Japanese Sword.   "Slightly curved steel blade.   Copper habaki.   Wood hilt covered with fish-skin and wrapped with cloth so as to expose skin partially. Black lacquered wood scabbard, oval section, with loop."

When re-written to accord with a syntax convention it reads: "Blade steel, slightly curved. Habaki copper. Hilt core wooden covered with fish-skin, partially wrapped with cloth. Scabbard wood, oval in section with loop, lacquered black."

The syntax convention introduces regularity of treatment to successive phrases, regardless of their content.   The principles are: each element of description relates to just one part of the object and the named part is the leading term (ie first word stated).   It is followed by the main descriptor, which in this case is considered to be the term describing the material of which that part is made, and each element concludes with an adjectival phrase that adds some qualification or minor detail. This design for comprehensible but concise presentation underlies the concept of a data element which is given a more formal meaning in the following chapters describing a framework for museum information. Within this syntax convention, an element can be stated concisely or expanded in moderation: there is no compelling rule.   In certain circumstances it may be reduced to the leading term or 'keyword' but if it is more fully expressed, priority within the word-order should be determined by diminishing importance.   Precedence should reflect the trend from general to particular, and from dominant to subordinate.

DATE CONVENTIONS

Alternative ways of expressing dates illustrate a fundamental point concerning the tendency to formalise statements of all kinds -- conventions should never interfere with the readable quality of information. Conventions designed to compress information may defeat that objective. For example, by reducing a date to six digits (09.01.85) there may be uncertainty whether the format applies the American or the European convention. The difference between these conventions is that the month is represented by the first two digits in the American form whereas the day-number occupies that position in the European form. Thus the coded date (09.01.85) represents September 1st, 1985 by American convention and 9th January 1985 by European convention. There is further possibility of confusion in a museum context (though not usually in a business environment) arising from the expression of the year by only two digits: this places a year only within its century but gives no indication of which century, eg '85 = 1885 or 1985?

Instead of using wholly numerical dates, some curators prefer to see the name of the month, either stated in full or abbreviated, eg

    9th January 1985   OR   9th Jan 1985   OR   09 Jan 1985

OR   January 9, 1985   OR   Jan. 09 1985   OR   1985 Jan 09.

When considering which of these alternative conventions to adopt, there are two factors to be reconciled so far as possible, for they are not entirely compatible (in manual systems). Is the format suitable for sorting? This question is concerned with the manipulation of dates, ie assembling records into order of date, commencing either with the earliest or with the most recent. This factor is of great practical significance, especially in computer-based systems where characteristics of the software may influence the decision. The other question concerns presentation: Which format is more readable? In the special context of public catalogues (particularly in catalogues for publication) a decision is normally taken on the preferred style to be adopted for dates. For example, '9th January 1985' may be preferred for documentation in the public domain.

In practice, some computer systems offer the best of both worlds and have considerable advantages of convenience over the expression of dates on manual records, where once typed a date is immutable except by erasure and re-typing. The versatile nature of computerised date recording is due to the fact that a translation can be effected between the sequence of characters typed at the keyboard and an unseen version in which the data are stored as an integer. This internal facility allows several forms of date to be input and recognised: all of them will be converted to the same value for storage. The following forms of entry, in addition to the coded version, are accepted as mixed input by one computer program known to the author (using upper and lower case indiscriminately):

19-MAR-86   19 MARCH 1986   19th March 1986

To complete this seemingly intelligent reception of dates, some computer systems enable conversion to be made at the time of output, that is to say, on retrieval of dates for display on screen or for printing as reports on paper.

For the purpose of recording dates, therefore, whether in preparation for input to computer or for purely manual records, a clear, unambiguous and consistent convention should be chosen. Obviously dates are treated as formal elements of information, (a point discussed in Chapter 6) in which a minimum requirement should be to express the year in full (4 digits) and the month probably in alphabetic form rather than as a numeric code (to avoid possible confusion with day-number). If names of months are to be used, it is desirable to adopt the abbreviated form and to standardise the number of characters (ie three) to avoid the variable lengths of names that would otherwise occur, eg March, April, May, June, Aug, Sept, etc. The use of Roman numerals for months is not appropriate. Syntax can be a matter of choice, considering the options to be:

DAY-MONTH-YEAR   MONTH-DAY-YEAR   YEAR-MONTH-DAY

Probably either the first (European) or the second (American) of these will be preferred but for manual sorting of cards the third version can be more effective.

It is a mistake to imagine that the exact formula used for dates in written documents for computer input actually determine the possibilities for sorting and retrieving them. As mentioned above, assuming that the date conversion facility is included in the computer software, a program performs these functions on the concealed internal format of dates by representing them as whole numbers. It manipulates dates in machine-readable form, including calculation of date intervals if needed, and converts them on output to humanly recognisable values.

PERSONAL NAME CONVENTIONS

So great is the variety of references made to persons, both living and historical, in museum records that it would be facile to suppose that one convention should regulate the form of all names. Conventions are indeed required for handling personal names but more than one may be required. The problem is comparable to that involving dates.

There are conventions for the form of names in ordinary speech and correspondence which come naturally to mind because that is the way we have learned to express them. However, when we refer to the telephone directory, other conventions apply because a different syntax is needed for sorting by surname. (Another convention would be needed if the phone directory was sequenced by forenames.) The facility to enable alphabetic listing of personal names is essential for many museum requirements and therefore an appropriate convention to permit sorting is of supreme importance and must often over-ride objections to the syntax that is necessary to effect it.

In every situation where we require a directory of personal names, eg owners, donors, makers, etc the most appropriate convention is to state the family name first, followed by the forenames (or their initials) of the person thus identified. However, the position of personal title deserves rather careful consideration because variations in syntax can produce forms of name in which title has at least three positions, eg

1. Revd. A C Brown
2. Brown, Revd. A C
3. Brown, A C; Revd.

Different conventions of punctuation are introduced in parallel with the alternative forms of syntax. The syntax of the last version is rather unnatural because it departs from the conventions of common speech but it complies perfectly with the requirements for a directory listing. We are conditioned to using a form of address in which the name of a person is normally preceded by his or her title. The second option looks acceptable as a compromise: in fact, it is the word order used in phone directories, where titles such as 'Revd' and 'Dr' are interpolated between the surname and the forenames or initials. In a system of that kind we should expect to find the following names in the order shown below:

    a. Brown, Revd. A C

    b. Brown, Miss Alice J

    c. Brown, Mr. Andrew B

    d. Brown, Mrs. Teresa A

    e. Brown, Major Thomas Headley

    f. Brown, Dr. William Arthur

This sequence seems logical to our conditioned minds because in reading it we ignore the lexical value of the title term (Revd., Major, Dr. etc) as if it did not exist.

Unfortunately strict logic does not produce the sequence (a-f) as above: the rules of alphabetic sorting demand that every character be scanned in turn and none be omitted. Thus, (following 'Brown') the title 'Dr.' precedes 'Major', which in turn precedes 'Miss' and this precedes 'Mr', 'Mrs' and 'Revd' in that order. Consequently if the names are allowed to remain in that form, with personal title following surname, the sequence is re-arranged by computer in the order below:

    f. Brown, Dr. William Arthur

    e. Brown, Major Thomas Headley

    b. Brown, Miss Alice J.

    c. Brown, Mr. Andrew B.

    d. Brown, Mrs. Teresa A.

    a. Brown, Revd. A C

We must acknowledge the unerring logic of the computer for alphabetic sorting. Therefore, to avoid creating the inept sequence (f-a) above, we have to adopt a convention placing title at the end, after all names.

When personal names are used in a context that does not require facility for directory listing then the natural order can be followed, starting with title (if required) and ending with the family name.

There is some advantage in stating the names of persons who are the subjects of portraits in this natural form: it avoids distorting the names of subjects whose public appellation is actually a title, eg 'Duke of Marlborough' and 'Queen of Tonga', etc. For reference to historical personages it is less contrived to use the normal form of a name except where their inclusion in a directory is essential, eg 'George Washington' not 'Washington, George; Mr.' and 'Emperor Haile Selassie' not 'Selassie, Haile; Emperor'. Names retained in the natural form can be individually retrieved by free-text search on those computer systems that offer this technique but clearly cannot usefully be listed. Of course, in sophisticated computer systems it is possible to store names in one form and to display them reconstructed in another. Such are the problems of sorting personal names and the reasons for establishing clear conventions to govern the form in which they are presented.

CONVENTIONS FOR INDEXING

Conventions are especially important in those sections of records that contain terms required for indexing. In a typical book index the alphabetical list of terms usually cites the occurrence of particular words and corresponding references to page numbers, eg

> catalogue, 2, 6, 38, 54, 93-5
>
> cataloguer, 3, 54
>
> cataloguing, 2, 6, 38
>
> .... in the Smithsonian 94-6
>
> .... of composite objects, 2-3

Alternatively, and frequently in modern textbooks, the index may give reference to topics selected and named by the indexer, the topic names being chosen to indicate the scope of the text rather than the actual occurrence of particular words, eg

> catalogue cards, 38
>
> catalogue duplicate, 95
>
> catalogue format, 54, 93-6
>
> catalogue methods, 2-6

This is actually a classified index indicating categories of subject matter instead of unique word occurrences. In naming categories, the selected term is standardised by disregarding variants (such as 'cataloguer' and 'cataloguing') and by not recording separately the singular and plural forms. This kind of index is often supplemented by an index of unique names such as for persons, products and places.

The indexes required for museum collections are of both kinds, those comparable with the classified index being appropriate wherever data can be standardised and those resembling word lists being retained where unique names, dates and reference numbers occur in the record. In the computer index, conventions must ensure that the terms entered into records exactly match the terms used in the index, because these act as finding aids for retrieving information. Under computer methods the terminology of the index has a dominant influence over the lexical form of data accepted but this is rarely the case with manual indices.

An important syntax convention in computerised systems, excepting those that store unstructured text, is to ensure that the operative term is the first word within the phrase to be indexed (to facilitate retrieval and sorting). This convention is referred to here as 'leading keyword'. The effects of using standard terms and leading keyword are illustrated in the following examples, but first these are shown without applying any such conventions. These phrases might occur in records reporting conservation treatment applied to a series of objects in the laboratory.

g.   air-dried by fan

h.   carbon tetrachloride applied by pipette

i.   dampness removed in warm air from fan

j.   degreased with C tetrachloride on sponge

k.   dehydrated by air-flow from fan

l.   desiccated over calcium chloride

m.   moisture extracted by absorbent pad

n.   silica gel applied to damp area

o.   solvent brushed on and removed by absorption

p.   stain removed by solvent on pad

Without conventions to control the expression of data, statements take the form of free-text narrative and their arrangement in alphabetic order serves no useful purpose: nor can data be retrieved by searching for specific terms unless every word be examined either visually or by electronic means. However, if a lexicon of accepted terms is introduced to bring some standardisation to the operative terms (keywords), we can then impose a convention which dictates that the keyword shall be the leading term in each expression. The phrases are now quite transformed and their usefulness enhanced because the result of alphabetic sorting is an organised index of a type called 'keyword and context' (KWAC), which is fully described in works on bibliographic cataloguing, eg Hunter & Bakewell, 1983. In the sorted list the entries appear as follows (corresponding examples from list above identified by letter):

m.   dehydrated using absorbent pad

l.   dehydrated using calcium chloride desiccator

k.   dehydrated using cold air-flow from fan

g.   dehydrated using hair-drier cool

i.   dehydrated using hair-drier warm

n.   dehydrated using silica gel pack

o.   solvent applied by brush and absorbed by tissue

p.   solvent applied on pad of cellulose tissue

h.   solvent carbon tetrachloride applied by pipette

j.   solvent carbon tetrachloride applied on sponge

CONVENTIONS ON PUNCTUATION

Apart from restrained use of normal punctuation in those parts of a record where clarity requires it, certain punctuation marks may be selected for special purposes as signals to infer some qualification of the data. Here it is best to choose symbols that do not have very specific meaning in their general application. For example, the dollar sign and the pound sign are as obviously unsuitable for special use (other than their monetary one) as the question mark would be.

Unfortunately, among the conventions chosen by the Museum Documentation Association, the ampersand and the 'equals' sign, were adopted for special use. Ampersand is used as a 'keyword separator' and this results in its insertion into phrases with alarming frequency, its effect then being to destroy all continuity; eg

Melbourne & Victoria & Australia

sandstone & red & calcareous

watercolour & English & Newcastle School

In ordinary usage the ampersand makes a link between proper names of
equal status, such as the partners in a company, eg "Messrs. Stone,
Fawdry & Stone, Ltd". The divergence of MDA conventions from those
involving the same symbols in general use makes them seem intrusive.
Unfortunate difficulties have been reported for the cataloguing of plant
and fossil specimens (Bainbridge, 1985; Gardiner and McClinton, 1985)
resulting from the Museum Documentation Association's use of round
brackets, ampersand and equals sign for acceptance of data into the
GOS computer system. The special meanings given to all three of these
symbols were found to be in conflict with the established international
conventions of biological nomenclature. This criticism amounts to more
than mere dislike of poorly chosen signs on cosmetic grounds.

The 'equals' sign is employed by MDA convention as a 'range
separator' to associate the lower and upper limits of a numeric series
such as a period of years, eg 1831=1909. This is in contrast to the
ordinary convention, using a hyphen for the same purpose, and gives
the appearance of a nonsensical arithmetic equation. In another context
reported by Thorpe (1984) relating to costume, it is incongruous to
read "waist = hem: length 104cm" or "underarm = elbow: length 30cm".
That author refers to the MDA system as like "working in code" and
maintains that "the more complicated characteristics of certain garments
... are rendered more clearly in free text than in code". This assertion
can be better appreciated by reference to description of a military
uniform jacket (from Mollo, 1985) which applies MDA conventions of
syntax and punctuation:-

*descg

*descn : components : body & collar & rank badge & cuff & cuff
slash & lace & shoulder cord & skirt slash & piping & button &
lining

*descn body

*aspect materials : wool cloth

* colour : scarlet

*descn collar

*aspect materials : wool cloth

* colour : blue

* shape : upright, open

* height : 2.50 in

*descn rank badge

*aspect materials : velvet, metal thread

* colour : red, gold and silver

*insc *pos front *meth embroidered

*descr within a silver laurel wreath, two red velvet crossed batons
picked out in gold (etc ...)

The above description just does not satisfy the desire for coherence
that some curators regard as paramount in usable records. A typical
reaction is expressed in the following statement (Smith, 1983) relating
to all examples of this format: "the highly structured arrangement of
the MDS cards .... broke up the essential information into so many
pieces that a clear and concise statement about the object could not be
taken in at a single glance."

All punctuation marks in the above example, (the asterisk, colon
and ampersand) have special meaning under conventions of the Museum
Documentation Association which are not self-evident to the uninitiated.
The confusing impact of these conventions is increased by their frequency. The authors of a recent textbook (Wood-Harper, Antill and
Avison, 1985) remark, "Mistakes can ... be made where the characters
to be typed do not follow the user's logic. An example of this occurs in
using many packages and programming languages where it is necessary
to use .... punctuation marks which do not follow the rules of natural
language."

Of course, special signs may be needed for various reasons, such
as to identify keywords in free-text and to separate elements within a
record but the insertion of appropriate symbols (if they are found to be
necessary) can be left until beginning the process of input to computer.
Indeed, the choice of symbols for these purposes is likely to be dictated
by whatever computer package is acquired for data-processing. (MDA
separator conventions are required for processing records by GOS).

Quite apart from considerations of computer technology, there may be need to mark certain components of text to indicate parcels of information inserted by the cataloguer which were not present in the original source. Possibly the most suitable signs on the keyboard for use in marking interpolated fact or comment are angle brackets <> and square brackets []. Quotation marks, oblique slash / and asterisks are to be avoided because they risk confusion with retrieval commands that operate under some computer systems. If additional signals are wanted, consider using the 'plus' sign (but in non-numeric contexts only), the exclamation mark or the superscript zero° (used for angular measure in 'degrees'), providing their emplacement in the text does not become too frequent.

ABBREVIATIONS AND CODES

Sets of abbreviations should be formulated for adoption in respect of dimensional units, personal titles, units of time, counties, states and nations by reference to established standard sources such as a world gazetteer, and published national/international standards such as ASA, BSI, DIN and SI. Coding goes a step further than abbreviation because it involves contracting the characters contained in a word by selective omission rather than by simple truncation: it produces WN (code for Wisconsin) in place of Wisc. (an abbreviation) and COLA for Columbia. Acronyms are also coded forms, eg SC for South Carolina, as are the geocodes proposed in Chapter 8, eg EQPA representing 'equatorial belt, Pacific sector'.

In more extreme form codes involve replacing words by numbers. This is useful when series of proper names must be presented in a prescribed order which is not alphabetical. This requirement arises when there is a need for a systematic arrangement, perhaps in addition to an index, as for example in creating a list of army regiments by order of precedence (Mollo, 1985). As Mollo says, "In the case of regimental titles, we are used to finding them in precedence order. To achieve this in a computer ... we have had to develop a *serv code". This allocates a serial number to each regiment named according to its position in the desired sequence.

A section of it looks like this: 120   Royal Artillery

121   Royal Engineers

122   Royal Flying Corps

123   Royal Signals

130   Foot Guards

130.1   Grenadier Guards

130.5   Welsh Guards

131   Infantry (etc ...)

The purpose of numerical codes is to regulate sorting so as to produce a schematic arrangement of terms independent of alphabetic position. The option then arises of citing the code in place of the proper name, as suggested in the article by Mollo. This substituted use of codes may be convenient to the cataloguer but it is as obscure to the user of the catalogue as if it had been created by encryption. The acceptable use of codes is as a device to aid sorting by computer, which can be programmed to print intelligible headings while the codes themselves remain unseen.

———————

REFERENCES

Bainbridge, J. (1985)   "The computerisation of herbarium records at Sunderland Museum" MDA Information vol.9 no.3 p.88-97.

Borko, H. and C.L.Berner (1978) "Indexing Concepts and Methods" New York & London: Academic Press Inc.   261pp.

Gardiner, T. and B. McClinton (1985) "Palaeontological documentation in the Ulster Museum" MDA Information vol.9 no.3 p.85-87.

Hunter, E. and K.G.B. Bakewell (1983) "Cataloguing" 2nd edn. London: Clive Bingley. New York: K.G. Saur.   222pp.

Mollo, B. (1985)   "The use of the computer for cataloguing at the National Army Museum" MDA Information vol.9 no.3 p.75-79.

Ramsden, M.J. (1974) "An Introduction to Index Language Construction: a programmed text"   London: Clive Bingley   206pp.

Smith, J.F. (1983) "Stamford Museum"
MDA Information vol 6, no 4, p.61.

Thorpe, Louise (1984)   "The MDA Costume card: users' meeting" MDA Information vol.8 no.3 (Oct) p.82-85.

Wood-Harper A.T., Lyn Antill and D.E.Avison (1985)
"Information Systems Definition: the multiview approach"
Oxford: Blackwell Scientific Press. 167pp.

Chapter 6

The reference framework

Record systems that are not regulated by control of vocabulary and not structured in their organisation still exist as survivals from the early days of museum collections. In modern times they have proved to be inadequate for the more extensive functions which museum records are now required to perform. This inadequacy has been emphasised in recent years by the advantages of record systems and catalogues held on computers. The advent of computing has injected a more rigorous form of discipline into all kinds of organisational tasks to which it has been applied and museum cataloguing is no exception. The power of computers to manipulate large amounts of information has opened up possibilities for access to selected parts of detailed records, whether constructed as textual documents or as file entries. In the museum context this offers the possibility of comparing, extracting and listing details that formerly remained locked in the individual objects' records. The price of this freedom to obtain information is the adoption of new standards in preparing records. In the library profession, where standards in cataloguing have emerged over many years and in which disciplined procedures are already in general practice, transfer to computerised systems has been less arduous than it is proving to be for museums.

When adopting disciplined methods of cataloguing, curators will be aware that the problem is not merely a question of improving standards henceforward but of revising all existing records retrospectively to make both old and new records amenable to the new technology. This problem has been rather overlooked in the exposition of methods by some advisory bodies, preoccupied in creating standards for writing new records rather than for converting old. It has simply been assumed that curators will rewrite their entire catalogues in conformity with new standards. Roberts (1985) remarks that "... if the organisation (of the original record) differs from the new standard, either the operator (at computer keyboard) or the curator may have to interpret the information prior to entry or the system will have to be used to carry out a standardisation process...", adding "These operations of interpretation and standardisation of an original record are analogous to the work involved in reprocessing (ie re-writing) existing manual records into a new manual format."

For the larger museums this approach to the problem is quite unrealistic: consequently improvement of current record standards will not touch the vast bulk of archival records. A framework for organising records in museums and similar collections must therefore be cast in generous terms to allow archival records to be manipulated by editing facilities on computer, without the necessity of rewriting them. While he provides exhaustive discussion of retrospective procedures for improving the documentation of an existing collection (by re-writing the records) Roberts concentrates his attention on the methods used for retrospective 'inventorying' and 'recataloguing'. He continues, ".....indexes may be derived from the newly-produced records resulting from ..... recataloguing programmes or from existing records if these are sufficiently well organised ...". The MDA publication from which these remarks are quoted offers no further elaboration of options available to pursue the latter possibility but this is surely the most feasible solution (if only as preliminary to more fundamental revision) for museums which are under-staffed, under-financed and under other pressures for the attention of curators. It must be the instinctive response of museum administrators to point to the formidable investment of money, time and

86

expertise represented by the accumulated documentary records relating to collections (and the doubtful cost/benefit justification of financing full-scale recataloguing).

A retrospective indexing programme to exploit the information within curatorial records is recognised to be one method of improving the standard of access to information in inherited records. What seems not to have been considered previously is the possibility of copying all such records to computer storage media and reformatting these by word-processing techniques in such a way as to permit automatic indexing of all significant terms for purposes of information retrieval. This solution has been ignored perhaps because records revised in this comparatively superficial manner cannot conform to the MDA standard unless they are edited so drastically as, in effect, to be re-written. By way of contrast it may be emphasised that records reformatted by word-processor can be brought within the framework described under the name REFORM in the following chapters. This is possible because the system to be described allows flexible conformity at two distinct levels represented respectively by Statements and Elements.

In the United Kingdom during a period of about a decade prior to the formation of the MDA there emerged an evident desire on the part of curators to construct a comprehensive range of recording media and to encourage a unified approach to the recording of museum objects (Lewis, 1967). The more direct aim was to produce standard printed cards for entering records into catalogue files. The possibility of using computers to manipulate these data was already apparent and this led to the formulation of an additional objective, to develop "a communication format" (Cutbill, Hallan and Lewis, 1971). This was intended to act as "a means of communicating between systems by machine" and envisaged involving the exchange of computer tapes of machine readable data. "The MCF (Museum Communication Format) can be used for holding data to be communicated between two otherwise incompatible systems. It can also be used as a tool for designing local input ...." "As a design tool it ensures that those designing local formats analyse their data to the same specification ...." Thus, it appears that from its origin as a standard for data transfer, the museum communication format later became an obligatory format for record creation. This objective has remained a dominant force in the promotion of documentation standards (in the broad sense) by the MDA throughout its ten-year history. Commendable as this aim is, the underlying assumption is questionable; namely, that the conceptual 'data standard' developed for the Sedgwick Museum project is necessarily the proper device for organising all museum data into suitable form for input to computer. This proposition can be fairly judged by reading a succinct account of the method used in structuring data for manipulation by the computer package that was devised and written specifically for this purpose (Porter, 1982).

How many users of the Museum Documentation System realise that the formula upon which it is founded was developed and completed some years before the MDA itself was established? In the words of its authors (Cutbill, Hallan and Lewis, 1971), "Much can be achieved at the cost of severe restrictions on vocabulary, grammar and syntax". It is unequivocally stated that the Museum Communication System (now better known as the Museum Documentation System) employs "a non-natural language with an artificial structure ..." and "an artificial grammar". It clearly over-estimated the willingness of the eventual user to abandon natural language and to analyse records into minutely defined fragments. It arose from a series of research projects at Cambridge University which focussed on the computerisation of records in the Sedgwick Museum of Geology. The concluding report, which had profound influence on the subsequent development of museum recording methods, confirms that "This early work on the communication format laid the foundation for the present Museum Documentation Standard" (Porter, Light and Roberts, 1976). A description of the fundamental nature of the 'data standard', a model for handling data on computer while retaining relationship between fragmented components of information, is included in that report (paragraph 5.5.2).

In essence this model is more closely connected with the theory of database (Information Technology) than with the subject matter of museum information. Actually, there is no intrinsic reason why its use should be confined to museums at all. As a computing study there is no doubt that the technique of data-processing developed at Cambridge during the period 1966-69 was innovative and valuable (cf. Cutbill and Williams, 1971). Remarkably, it bears a superficial resemblance to the equally appropriate computer operating system originated at almost exactly the same time in the United States by Richard Pick and now widely known throughout the computing world under his name. This also began as a special-purpose project (it was supplied to the U.S. Army in 1969 as GIM, 'General Information Management') but soon afterwards found a wider application as a database for the commercial market, where it became firmly established during the years 1973-1976.

It was at the end of the Sedgwick Museum project in December 1976 that the Museum Association's own voluntary committees of curators working under the umbrella of the Information Retrieval Group (IRGMA) decided to relinquish independent ambitions and to act in an advisory capacity to the newly formed Museum Documentation Association. Simultaneously, the appointment of former members of the Sedgwick team as the nucleus of full-time staff at the MDA ensured its inheritance of the data-processing concepts and techniques pioneered by the research study.

Some justification for offering an alternative model for compiling object records springs from the knowledge that there are numerous museums and galleries in the United Kingdom and elsewhere that have retarded their plans to improve documentation while searching for a framework which allows them to influence the design and style of their records. The caution being exercised in these institutions reflects their fundamental concern to determine for themselves the form in which their information is expressed in various types of record and in the resultant catalogues.

A reference framework for organising museum records that meets these qualifications has been developed by studying and analysing the informational content of a wide range of catalogues and museum inventories. By making a survey of the topics encountered (some more regularly than others) in all kinds of museum record, the concepts embodied in the data are more clearly appreciated. This leads to recognition of a number of statements which can be identified repeatedly in object records of every type and format, textual and structured.

FORMAL DEFINITION

The information that is specified for records relating to collected objects is expressed according to different formulae in various countries, influenced by their preferred definitions and by distinctive views of relationships between component facets of information. To illustrate this point, we might reflect on the contrasting patterns of information normally contributing to a museum record in the form approved by the French Directorate of Museums, the Australian Gallery Directors' Council and the Canadian Heritage Information Network respectively. The fluidity of definition that is evident in any such survey encourages me to believe that there is room for additional proposals. The publication of REFORM is intended to augment and assist the evolution of catalogue and control documentation, not only in institutional museums but also in privately owned collections of artefacts, memorabilia and ephemera.

From this point onwards the 'reference framework' to be described is a definitive model which is known by the acronym REFORM *.

[*REFORM = REference Framework for Organising Records in Museums.]

Topics previously mentioned and illustrated from actual examples in Chapters 2 and 3 are now designated as Statements. Each Statement is a natural expression relating to a single topic, such as Acquisition or Discovery, which can be partitioned into smaller segments here called Elements. Within the reference framework each Statement occupies a Section which can be regarded as a filing box. The cabinets that hold all these Sections, together with the files of Statements they contain, comprise the reference framework. In the REFORM structure, file-boxes (Sections) are stacked in four tiers and it is an advantage to stabilise their arrangement to establish relationship between files by proximity.

REFORM is a modular construction and new Sections can be added if necessary, providing that they do not duplicate (even partially) those Sections already present. While bearing in mind its potential for expansion, the model of REFORM given in this and following chapters is believed to be comprehensive. Certainly it provides a very extensive and flexible museum information system. The following Statements occurring in museum records already examined must be analysed in turn to establish how we may accommodate them in the reference model.

Always present: an Acquisition Statement

an Identity Statement

a Statement of Origin

a Description Statement

a Classification Statement

There may also be: Statement of Ownerships

a Statement of Association

a Discovery Statement

an Inscription Statement

an Imagery Statement

In records oriented towards collection management there can be:

a Status Statement

a Location Statement

a Valuation Statement

a Loan Statement

less regularly occurring:

a Conservation Statement

an Exhibition Statement

an Attribution Statement

a Citation Statement

a Facsimile Statement

a Derivation Statement

a Function Statement

a Biography Statement

Each of these topics may be subjected to more detailed analysis by applying a question-and-answer technique to enumerate the individual facts contained within the Statement and to itemize what is known about a given museum object (see 'Defining Elements', p.95). However, it is not obligatory to pursue the analysis of each Statement with the intent of extracting the constituent facts as separate Elements: the analysis can be regarded as a method for checking that all the requisite facts have been included in a textual Statement. In adopting this procedure, the museum can claim to observe the conceptual structure defined by the reference framework although implementing it in textual records

91

divided simply into paragraphs, each of which represents a Statement named in REFORM.

If records are structured only to this extent (ie at the paragraph level) it is possible to transfer them to computer storage but naturally to search these files requires a special kind of computer software known as a text storage and retrieval system (cf Chapter 12). If this approach is taken, it is still important to observe the fully elaborated definitions of the Statements comprising the model record. This is necessary to avoid indistinct boundaries between Sections and to ensure that what is included in each Section does not diverge between one department (or institution) and another. If, as a matter of routine, all information about objects is recorded consistently in a series of paragraphs under these headings, reference to details becomes very much simpler than in unstructured text. However, cross-reference between records and comparison of corresponding particulars of discrete objects is not improved to the extent that is possible in records that are structured as a series of Elements.

The benefit secured by retaining the integrity of Statements is the easy readability of narrative syntax but the penalty is that a paragraph becomes the smallest unit that can be isolated in answer to a question. While it is convenient for some purposes to read elements of fact in the context of other information about an object, in other situations this is less important than the comparison of corresponding facts about a series of objects. In the latter situation the advantage lies with records that are structured as series of Elements. The component Elements may be named, numbered, marked or merely separated but in effect they can be isolated either visually (on card records) or by active processing (on computer) as required. Structuring by paragraph allows only partial application of REFORM (Statement-based) but the choice remains with the user: the more versatile application of REFORM is Element-based.

A FOUR-TIERED STRUCTURE

Statements are the primary divisions of a record and their constitution is explained in this chapter. The secondary divisions (ie definition of the Elements within each Statement) are examined in following chapters.

Before turning to the question of definitions, a comment is needed on the relationship of Statements, one to another, which is shown by the positions they occupy in the framework. Some of the information about an object is <u>historical</u>, in the sense that it reports events which involved that object up to and including its acquisition by the museum (but not including any subsequent events during the custodianship of the museum). We can bracket together as historical information everything included in Statements describing Origin, Ownership, Association, Discovery, Function, Derivation and Acquisition; these form the basal First Tier of the REFORM structure.

Then there is information which is <u>descriptive</u> of the object itself, and which is timeless in the sense that its content is not related to the object's history but to its physical attributes. Statements of the object's Identity, Description, Marks, Inscription, and Imagery are of this type and Classification is closely related to these characteristics. These comprise the Second Tier of REFORM.

There is another kind of information about collected objects which results from exhibiting, inspecting and interpreting the objects. In simple terms the resulting statements report investigations and incidents which ensure that museum objects are preserved, recognised and appreciated: these are Statements on Conservation, Exhibition, Attribution, Citation and Facsimile. They hold information that is event-based and which form the Third Tier of REFORM.

From the cataloguer's viewpoint these Sections contain data which are supplemented on repeated occasions, every time a new report is filed. They hold data that is event-based. These data are <u>cumulative</u> because existing Statements that are already on file for Conservation, Exhibition, Attribution, etc do not become irrelevant when new information is added. Thus, when a ceramic vase is sent to the laboratory for restoration, its treatment is noted in a Conservation Statement. On each subsequent occasion when that vase is examined by a conservator he/she will know from the record what treatment was previously applied to the object and each additional process used must be documented by adding to the information already on file. So the Conservation Section of any record accommodates several Statements each of different date.

Similarly in the Section on Exhibition, Statements contain details of every exhibition in which, say, a given sculpture has been shown. The information remains pertinent to the record indefinitely (for a work of art especially) and is not discarded when the event is concluded. The same considerations apply with reference to both Citation and Facsimile Statements: the data expands as citations come to light and as new references and reproductions are published. The old information does not become obsolete: these Sections of the record are cumulative.

Lastly, the Fourth Tier comprises information needed to support effective measures for managing collections. These managerial data are also concerned with incidents which may be repeated at any time but the nature of the data is predominantly practical, concerning movements of objects (eg from storage to conservation, etc), also valuations for insurance and periodic assessments of condition or other aspects. Such data are held in Statements on current Status, Location, Valuation and Loans. In contrast to Statements of the Third Tier, with managerial data the curator is interested only in the current position and, when a change is made in current data, the previous Statement becomes redundant and may be cleared from that Section.

Thus, if an item is released on loan to another institution the details are entered in a Loan Statement but when it is returned to the lender it serves no purpose to retain this data, except possibly in case damage to the object is detected and a claim has to be made on insurers. As a precaution, therefore, the data can remain on file until the next loan of the same object is made and at that time the data on the preceding borrower can be deleted. The same principle applies to the other Sections in this group. When a curator decides that the Status of an object needs to be changed to indicate the latest review of some aspect, he substitutes the new assessment. For example, if an object is found to be damaged but is not immediately repaired, the Statement will record its condition as 'damaged' (with details) and that fact replaces the previous statement on its undamaged condition. Statements of the Fourth Tier are therefore dynamic and liable to change.

Of those topics identified in preceding chapters and included in the list on page 91 only Biography has been omitted from the model of REFORM presented here. Biographic statements are excluded on the grounds that by definition they do not refer to "an object" but actually to "a person" who is or was associated with the object in some way. Logic dictates therefore that biography does not form an intrinsic part of an object's record: details of a person's life unconnected with the object are a subject for independent records. This is a proper conclusion in theory and it is inescapable in practice because the inclusion of biographical information would add bulk to many records while merely repeating common data referring to the life of the artist or benefactor.

DEFINING ELEMENTS

On close inspection it is clear that any Statement can be partitioned into a number of segments, each presenting a single fact which cannot be further divided without losing something of its implication. Each segment of information that can be extracted from a Statement while retaining a meaningful relation to the object is called an Element. An Element can be characterised as the answer to a specific question and this is the basis of a method for defining every Element individually. The questions that may be asked on any topic depend on our use of just six interrogative words:

what?   where?   when?   who?   how?   why?

Every Element must relate to one or another of these forms of question.

Elements answering 'WHAT' relate to ITEMS or things;

"	"	'WHERE'	"	SITE or position;
"	"	'WHEN'	"	TIME;
"	"	'WHO'	"	PERSONS
"	"	'HOW'	"	ROLE or method
"	"	'WHY'	"	PURPOSE.

A list of questions arranged under these categories makes it easy to locate the appropriate Element within the reference framework (see Appendix I). In relation to any Statement, it is generally found that each of the six questions can be asked at least once in order to extract from it the constituent Elements. For example, let us analyse the Discovery Statement concerning the Assyrian Slab (Example 7):

95

"Stone Slab ... from the Temple of Nabu at Nineveh, ..." re-discovered in 1904 and finally cleared in 1927-8, the excavations being carried out by Dr. R. Campbell Thompson and others"

What was the ITEM discovered?	(the) Stone slab
Where was the SITE of discovery?	Temple of Nabu at Nineveh
When was the TIME of its discovery?	between 1904 and 1928
Which PERSON discovered it?	Dr. R Campbell Thompson
In what ROLE did he find it?	(as) excavator

PURPOSE is not applicable in this case: (in fact its use is rare). In some cases the answer to one question provokes another: this leads to recognition of secondary or dependent Elements, as illustrated from Example 23, the sculpture by Giacomo Zoffoli. Here we can analyse the Acquisition Statement as follows:

From which PERSON was it acquired?	David Peel & Co.Ltd.
In what ROLE did the company act?	(as) vendor
Where were they in business? (SITE)	2 Carlos Place, Mount Street, London
When was it acquired? (TIME)	May 1971
How was it acquired?	purchased
What price (ITEM/thing) was paid?	(say) £500

Relating to price, there are two dependent questions:

What grant (ITEM) was received?	(say) £250
Who (what PERSON) gave the grant?	Victoria & Albert Museum

By applying the same suite of questions to the subject-matter of every Statement in the context of various examples, a standard set of Elements can be established relating to each Statement. These are then formally recognised as components of the reference framework and each of them is referenced by a unique number. The number given to an Element is composed of three digits separated by stops, eg '3.2.1'.

The first digit identifies the relevant Tier of REFORM; (= Tier 3) The second digit identifies the number of the Section in that Tier (= Section 2) to which the Statement belongs. The third digit identifies the Element within that Statement; (= Element 1). Every segment of information that could be available for an object, therefore, is uniquely referenced by Element number and filed in the relevant Section.

EXPRESSING ELEMENTS

The exact form in which information is expressed within an Element is not dictated by REFORM: it is at this point that conventions generated in individual museums may take effect. Data may be written concisely or, if preferred, at length; either in accordance with a specified order of words or without constraints on syntax; with leading keyword or with keywords identified throughout the text. Choice of conventions is at the discretion of every user applying REFORM to collection records: conventions may be tailored to suit local circumstances and special requirements (perhaps for computer systems).

To determine the most suitable guidelines for preparing data and compiling each Element, the user of REFORM must define the museum's requirements in substantial detail and with a measure of foresight. To assist in the recognition of these objectives, the principal issues are discussed in Chapter 11. Before the reader confronts decisions on how individual Elements should be treated, it may be helpful to illustrate some of the various modes in which data can be written so that their respective limitations and potential can be seen. If an Element is treated as a textual expression then practically no constraints are imposed on the form of statement except that some effort to record facts concisely is desirable (see Example 31 in Chapter 5).

In describing the method and medium used in surface decoration of the Spode plate (Example 25), the textual mode produces an expression such as "blue transfer-printed underglaze decoration ... join visible at centre bottom of border". Being purely textual, no special word order has been imposed and the resulting statement is adequate for purposes of report, ie for providing an answer to the question, "What method of surface decoration was applied to this plate?". However, it has to be realised that this version would not be suitable for inclusion in an alphabetic listing of comments recorded under 'surface decoration'. The sentence would appear in that sequence alphabetically under "blue" but colour is probably not considered to be the most important aspect of its decoration. It would not be accessible for retrieval by the terms "transfer" or "underglaze" unless it is stored in a computer system designed for free-text search, in which a word at any position in a line or paragraph can be matched by automatic scanning of the entire text.

Taking an illustration from Example 8, describing a broadsword, consider the Element expressing its Association with a famous Person (Element 1.3.1). In textual mode this might be rendered as "Gill's blades were tested on a machine invented by Matthew Boulton". This too serves adequately for purposes of report in answering the question, "What personal association is known relating to this sword?". However, it does not lend itself to the requirements for listing, in this case by name, because the name of the associated person (Boulton) is not stated as the leading term: in fact the first-named person is the manufacturer.

If an Element is subject to a syntax convention which insists that the leading term is the (sole) keyword then it is suitable for inclusion in an alphabetic directory (eg personal names) as an aid to retrieval. Referring to Example 10 (The Water Mill), particularly to the Attribution of the painting, we might revise the Element stating the expert opinion so as to make it possible to retrieve all attributions in which the authenticity was confirmed. The opinion of Dr. H de Groot could be expressed by the following clause, "certified as a work by Hobbema (a genuine and characteristic work)". This introduces an organised word order, placing the critical term first, but it does not intrude on the natural style of expression nor does it curtail its length (the expert's words are quoted in parentheses). As well as serving the purpose of reporting, this makes the Element available to search and retrieval procedures based on the leading term. Only the extended length of the clause (which is not obligatory) may be inconvenient if comparative listing of attributions for several works is attempted.

A more restrictive convention limits the Element to a specified number of words (or characters). If these are reasonably few, (eg a maximum of 25 characters) this enables the entire phrase to act as a keyword which can be indexed and manipulated by computer for listing and matching. Returning to Example 25 (the Spode plate), under this convention the Element for Surface Decoration would be limited to "underglaze transfer blue" or "blue underglaze transfer", the word order being subject to rules determined locally. The benefits accruing from this self-imposed discipline include facility to list information about

98

surface decoration in comparable form for any number of ceramic items; also to retrieve by leading keyword. A convention on word order with defined priority for surname, forenames, title, honours, etc is needed for most Elements dealing with personal names because it enables both retrieval of individually specified entries and listing of all entries within a space-limited format.

The last and most formal syntax convention that can be applied dictates not only the length of the Element but also the incidence of punctuation, spaces and character type (numeric or letter). The strict control achieved by this method regulates the form of data that can be accepted to such an extent that in the extreme case it can be regarded as coded, as exemplified by the Geo-code devised for geographical classification (Element 2.2.1). Dates are treated under tight conventions in order to ensure that they can be handled in a predictable manner by computer. This still allows several possible styles for the presentation of dates. (There may be as many as ten date Elements in extensive records, some of which may require different styles.)

At the risk of repeating these points, we can examine the effect produced on the expression of an Element by treating the same data in each of these modes in turn. Firstly, consider a descriptive Element treated in free-text mode:

(A 1)   "three-branched, wall-mounted candelabrum, supported on an elaborate plaque bearing richly ornamented brackets, each with one candle-holder"

Assuming that terminology is controlled by lexicon, (and that the word 'candelabrum' is transferred to the classified name Element) the same material can be edited, without imposing a definite limit on length, and re-arranged to comply with the leading keyword convention thus:

(A 2)   "bracket, three-branched from an elaborate plaque".

This compares with another described in the following terms:

"pendant, five-branched, each with 12 candle-holders".

This assists both visual and computerised search of the leading term in all records containing this Element, eg to select those matching

99

the word 'bracket'. Even manual records filed on cards are improved by such conventions. Under the control of a lexicon, other keywords may include 'pendant', 'upright' (table candelabra), 'standard', etc.

As an alternative, the same data can be condensed into an Element of fixed length, the actual length being (let us say) 16 characters:

(A 3)   "bracket 3-branch"
               "pendant 60-light"

Lastly, there remains the option of presenting the data in a formal mode, which involves partitioning of the allotted space to accept data such as abbreviations and numerical characters in prescribed positions:

(A 4)   "BRAC/3BR/03L"   (12 characters)
               "PEND/5BR/60L"   ("   )

In this example, the first four characters represent an abbreviation for the keyword (type of candelabrum) followed by an oblique slash; the next three characters give the number of branches (BR) followed by an oblique slash; and the final three characters give the total number of candleholders (using L for lux or lights).

Clearly, these are progressive stages of increasing control exerted over the expression of information. Indeed they exemplify the imposition of structuring in various degrees not merely on the record as a whole but on every Element within the record. Most curators might agree that the last of these choices is least appropriate for such descriptive data because it is highly constrained. However, by way of contrast, there are other Elements for which a formal mode would be the usual choice: the representation of dates is a case in point. The following sequence gives exactly comparable treatments of information on dates, corresponding with the modes of presentation in (A 1) to (A 4) above.

(B 1)   Treatment of a date as free-text produces something like:
          "it was the twenty-fifth day in the month of September, the
          year of the incident being 1910"

(B 2)   Under the leading keyword convention, with year as keyword,
          we may write: "1910, September the twenty-fifth"

(B 3)   Further compression is needed to fit a fixed length mode, eg:
1910, Sept. 25th   (16   characters   including   spaces)   or
1910, September.

Syntax conventions can control the relative positions of year, month, day (eg in that order) but note that without additional conventions on abbreviation, word-length and punctuation the actual position of day-number is variable because it follows names of months which vary in length, eg:

1910, Sept. 1st

1910, June 1st

1910, May 1st

(B 4)   To adopt a fully formal mode for date, the number of spaces allocated to year, month and day must be defined, eg:

1910 Sep 25th

1911 May   3rd

In this case, the first four characters are defined as numerical values (year) followed by an obligatory space; the next three are the first 3 letters in the name of the month followed by one space (or two spaces if the day is less than the tenth); last comes the day of the month in ordinal form (one or two numerals and two alphabetic characters). In the formal mode at its logical extreme the date is coded, eg 1910/09/25. A code convention is habitually used in this context and being generally understood, it is accepted as a normal form for expressing dates.

In summary, therefore, Elements may be designated for treatment as (1) free-text, (2) variable length with leading keyword, (3) fixed length with syntax rules, (4) fixed length with character rules (analogous to rules of grammar). Options to manipulate data depend directly on the package of conventions chosen. In the following synopsis of these modes, reference to passive retrieval means that data residing in an Element cannot be addressed by content but can be recalled using keywords contained in other Elements of the record. Active retrieval means that data in an Element are directly accessible to searches based on the leading term (or phrase) or if the Element is formal, based on its entire content. Sorting means the facility to re-arrange data in alphabetic or numeric sequence. This results in the creation of a directory, eg of personal names, where individual entries within an

Element are unique (non-duplicating). Otherwise, where the same data are common to several records, the sorting process results in the grouping of entries for which the data in that Element are identical. To use an Element as a criterion for selecting records that share the same attribute, it must contain common data expressed in exactly similar form, ie it must be subject to the consistent application of conventions.

SUMMARY: RETRIEVAL   PROPERTIES   OF   DATA   ELEMENTS

(1) Free-text enables: passive recall of data for report;
active retrieval using word-search or inverted-
list facility (automatic word indexing);
output formatted by paragraph or document.

(2) Leading keyword: passive recall of data (optional);
active retrieval by leading keyword;
sorting by keyword;
retrieval by any significant term using
word-search or inverted-list facility;
output formatted subject to variable length.

(3) Fixed length passive recall of data (optional);
active retrieval by whole or part key term;
sorting by full text within limits;
output formatted by listing and tabulation;
grouping and sub-grouping by key terms.

(4) Formal Elements: active retrieval by whole or part data
and by character at any fixed position;
output formatted by listing and tabulation;
grouping and sub-grouping by common codes;
ideal for sorting by unique codes.

102

REFERENCES

Aubert,M. and D.Piot (1986) "Documenting French Cultural Property" Chapter 23 in Museum Documentation Systems edited by R.B.Light, D.A.Roberts and J.D. Stewart.

Cutbill,J.L. (ed) (1971) "Data Processing in Biology and Geology" Systematics Association Special Volume 3; London: Academic Press. 346 pp.

Cutbill,J.L., A.J.Hallan and G.D.Lewis (1971) "A Format for the machine exchange of museum data." in Data Processing in Biology and Geology edited by J.L. Cutbill. p255-274.

Cutbill,J.L. and D.B.Williams (1971) "A Program Package for Experimental Data Banking" (in) Data processing in Biology and Geology, edited by J.L. Cutbill. p105-113.

Lewis,G.D. (1967) "Information Retrieval for Museums" Museums Journal vol. 67 (2), p 88 - 91.

Light,R.B., D.A.Roberts and J.D. Stewart (eds) (1986) "Museum Documentation Systems: Applications and Developments" Boston, USA; London, UK; etc: Butterworths. 332pp.

Loy,T. (1986) "Collections computerization at the British Columbia Provincial Museum" Chapter 3 in R.B.Light et al. (eds).

Porter,M.F. (1982) "GOS: a package for making catalogues". Information Technology: Research and Development vol.1 pp.113-129.

Porter,M.F., R.B.Light and D.A. Roberts (1976) "A unified approach
    to the computerisation of museum catalogues." London:
    British Library. Research and Development Rept. 5338HC.

Sledge,J. and B.Comstock (1986) "The Canadian Heritage Information
    Network." Chapter 2 in R.B.Light et al. (eds).

Varveris,T. (1986) "A Documentation System for Australian Art Museums"
    Chapter 29 in R.B.Light et al. (eds).

Chapter 7

Historical data

In the broadest terms historical data summarise everything that happens
to an object up to (and including) its acquisition by a museum. This is
a clear definition by which we can associate all information comprising
the First Tier of the reference framework REFORM. None of the First-
Tier Sections actually identify or describe the object (this being the
role of Second-Tier Sections) but they are indispensible to many aspects
of a catalogue. The meaning of the museological concept 'provenance'
varies considerably between subject areas and this makes it unsuitable
as a term for general use.

Provenance implicates various aspects of an object's historical
record which can be separated in an analytical approach. For archaeo-
logists provenance usually denotes the circumstantial details about an
object's original discovery. In an art catalogue the term can cover not
only a sequence of previous owners with or without dates of transfer,
but also auction records, bequests and the source of its presentation or
loan. The sectional structure of REFORM provides a more discriminating
method of recording these historical particulars, by relating them with
the concepts of Acquisition, Ownership and Association. Details of an
object's presentation to the museum (or purchase) comprise a Statement
of Acquisition (Section 1.1.0) while details of previous owners and
bequests belong in Section 1.2.0. References to an object's appearance

in sale-rooms or in auction catalogues qualify as records of associated events, each of them a Statement of Association (Section 1.3.0).

Acquisition, origin and discovery are unique events but, by contrast, each incidence of ownership or association generates a new Statement so these Sections must accommodate multiple occurrences of every Element they contain, eg date, person, event, etc.

THE ACQUISITION STATEMENT   [Section   1.1.0]
The Acquisition Statement provides a record of the source from which the object came into the museum's possession and the terms that enabled the transfer of ownership to take place. A strict logic is maintained in relation to the matters recorded under acquisition: only the parties to the transfer of ownership or custodianship are relevant to this Section. All events preceding final transfer to the museum are excluded from the Acquisition Statement but may be included in the Statement on previous Owners [Section 1.2.0] and under Association [1.3.0] as appropriate.

1.1.1   The central Element of the Acquisition Statement is the name of the person or company from whom the object was acquired. This includes names of donors of items that were either presented or bequeathed, vendor's name for items which were purchased by the museum, and name of the auction house if bought at auction. In the latter situation, the private owner who submitted the object for sale by auction is not recorded as a party to the museum's acquisition; (the name of that owner will be entered in Section 1.2.0).

When a long-term or quasi-permanent loan is accepted, the object can be considered an acquisition in the sense that the museum accepts the responsibilities of curatorship from its legal owner. In such cases the object is given an Accession Number. For short-term loans of finite duration, not exceeding 2 years, customary registration practice varies among museums. Many do not regard such objects as acquisitions and therefore they are not given Accession Numbers but are simply insured and registered as inward Loans [Section 4.4.0] with an accompanying Statement of Valuation [Section 4.2.0].

1.1.2   As an acquisition can be transacted in a variety of ways, it is necessary to specify the method by which the object was

106

acquired. This is the function of Element 1.1.2. The acquisition process can be characterised by any of the following terms: 'purchase','auction', 'bequest' (presented posthumously on the donor's instruction), 'gift' (presented during the donor's life-time), 'loan' (for accessioned loans only, as per paragraph preceding). Entry of one of these terms should be a mandatory step in the creation of the Acquisition Statement.

1.1.3   The address of the person or company participating in the transaction (or from whom the object was received) is recorded for possible use in future communication (see Element 1.1.8 below).

1.1.4   If an object is purchased the price paid to the vendor is stated but otherwise this Element is not applicable,

1.1.5   When the Museum's funds are supplemented by grant-in-aid, the name of the source of additional finance is recorded (1.1.5) and also the amount of the contribution granted (Element 1.1.6). There may be more than one such grant contributing to the cost of a major purchase and each of them is recorded in a separate 'grant' Element of the Acquisition Statement.

1.1.7   As with all transactions, the date of acquisition is important. In this Element is recorded the date of the contract of sale to the museum or, otherwise, the date on which the museum took possession.

1.1.8   Finally, the nature of any conditions or special terms imposed by the benefactor or vendor must be recorded, as these may limit in some way the museum's freedom of action, either in exhibiting the object or in case of an intention to dispose of it subsequently.

THE STATEMENT ON OWNERSHIP   [Section   1.2.0]
The previous ownership of an object is part of its history and, in various ways, can often illuminate the significance of a piece either within a subject of study, or within the social or environmental context to which it belonged.   The item may be a simple domestic implement of little monetary value or it may be a highly desirable article sought by collectors: in both of these dissimilar circumstances the names of past owners are of considerable interest.   In the first case, the owner probably used the implement as a means of livelihood or in some aspect of social and domestic life.   Knowledge of successive ownerships adds

to our understanding of the historical period during which such articles were in use and, in a quite separate role, may support research into family history. In the case of a valuable article, the previous owners were probably collectors themselves and the history of their ownership contributes to a history of collecting. Perhaps some former owners had reputations as discerning collectors and to know that the object was previously in their possession is itself a factor adding significance and even value to the article.

Clearly, information may be available about the identity of several past owners and for each of them a separate Statement of Ownership is written, including data in the following Elements in each case:

1.2.1   The owner's name should be stated in a form governed by the chosen convention on personal names. By observing this practice it becomes feasible to sort names into alphabetic sequence and to search for individual names for the retrieval of associated information.

1.2.2   The method by which that owner acquired the object is sometimes known and should be recorded for its relevance in historical studies of the type already mentioned. It should be expressed by choosing the appropriate term from a limited vocabulary, eg 'inherited', 'bought', 'seized', 'commissioned', etc.

1.2.3   The place where the object was kept, used or exhibited, if known, should be stated and explanatory terms of that kind may be added as trailing data, ie appended to the locational Element.

1.2.4   The period of the person's ownership or such dates as are known, are included in a form suited either merely for reporting or, if desired, according to conventions which allow sorting by date order. Available options include: (a) restriction to year dates only, to be stated as a range (eg 1770-1780) allowing null dates where unknown (eg 1770-0000); (b) standard date with a suffix code indicating the acquisition (code A) of the object by that owner, disposal by that owner (code D) or in the possession of that owner (code P) at that date. Mixed conventions for dates, of course, render the information inaccessible to search and sorting by computer although it remains retrievable for report by means of associated Elements. (cf Example 35 and following discussion in Chapter 12.)

1.2.5   In some cases it is useful to record the name of a person to whom the object was transferred by the owner or from whom the owner obtained it. This Element also permits reference to a person not identified by name but indicated by position, function or relationship to the owner, eg (given) "to his nephew" or (bought) "from the village blacksmith".

When an object is acquired by the museum through the agency of an auction house or other intermediary, the last owner is named in this Section. If the object is received directly from its owner, either as a gift or by purchase, then the owner is already named in the Acquisition Statement. It is not necessary to repeat this information in a Statement of Ownership unless associated details are available for other Elements included in this Section.

THE STATEMENT OF ASSOCIATION   [Section   1.3.0]

There are numerous incidents in the history of an object that can associate it with persons other than by ownership. These include direct or intimate association as, for example, when a costume was "worn by (a named person)" and alternatively, association in which the connection is merely circumstantial, eg official robes worn at a particular event; or a dinner service used at an official reception.

Often an event in the life of a former owner is implicated but events themselves can be worthy of reference without linkage to any individual person, eg (of weapons) "captured at the battle of ....". Objects may be associated with places even without reference to events or persons, as in stating "the table was formerly at Brereton Hall". Undoubtedly, there are narrative statements in textual records that defeat the provisions of other recording schemes but which are readily accommodated in REFORM, as illustrated in the following extract:

"Together with this (flute) is an agreement between Mark Brace, a coal miner, of Newbridge and the Celynen Philharmonic Society, dated November 12th 1881, to pay ninepence a week towards the (cost of) flute until half the value of the instrument was paid."

Here we have association of an object with (i) a person, (ii) a place, (iii) a society, (iv) a date, and (v) text of interest as a social record.

With this example in mind, the Elements needed in every Statement of Association can be defined in the following terms:

1.3.1   The name of the person associated with the object must be given using the museum's chosen convention for personal names. This Element has a potentially broad and useful role in capturing data relating to diverse forms of association. In essence, if the person is not identifiable as a former owner, finder, maker or user it is likely that the relationship with the object should be treated as 'association'.

Groups of persons can be included and, if (as individuals) they are anonymous, they can be named as an organised body, for example a military regiment. This may be a repeating Element if synonyms have to be accommodated: eg if the object is a military button the associated regiment may have had changes of name during its history, as in the case of the 72nd Regiment of Foot, later the Seaforth Highlanders, also known as the Duke of Albany's Own Highlanders and sometimes as the 'Ross-shire Buffs'.

1.3.2   The name of any historical event in which the object was involved is entered in this Element.

1.3.3   The place with which the object is directly associated (excluding place of manufacture and place of discovery) should be recorded here, eg where the historical event occurred; or, in lieu of this, name of the place of abode or place of activity of the associated person (1.3.1).

1.3.4   The date of the association is required to establish, if possible, its historical position but date can be omitted (if not known) when a specific person or place has been named.

1.3.5   This Element gives a narrative explanation of the nature of the association between the object and the person, place or event. This should be concisely expressed but is not subject to constraints on syntax. At its simplest it may state: "given by her father", connecting "on the occasion of her wedding to Mr John Driver" in Element (1.3.2). In a quite different example, of a watercolour drawing of stained glass window panels, the narrative Element (1.3.5) records that they were "installed as clerestory windows", "at Tamworth Church" (1.3.3).

110

1.3.6　　This Element is for reference to Associated Pieces, ie separate items within the museum's collections which, together with the object presently described, constitute a 'set' or 'suite' (whichever expression is more appropriate in the particular context). For example, it may collate a set of clothes that were worn as an ensemble when each garment is registered under a different number, ie it provides cross-reference to a pair of shoes worn with a particular dress. Associated pieces of furniture are those which together furnished the same room in their former location. It is not necessary (or advisable) to include here other objects merely because they originate from the same maker: these can be related by Maker's Name from the Statement on Origin. Element (1.3.6) is independent of those preceding it in this Section and has a variety of uses.

1.3.7　　Taking a broader view of association, it may be treated as the cultural environment or context in which the object existed. Typically, in Archaeology, context includes names of cultures revealed through traditions and techniques of craftmanship: eg 'Maglemosian', 'Acheulian'. With reference to classical sites, the cultural context is the name of the colonial power, eg Greek, Roman, Etruscan, Parthian (the territorial position of a site is recorded under geographical class, eg Basilicata). In Ethnography, cultural context is described by tribal name, which of course is usually quite distinct from territorial names. In Social History and Art the cultural context is a stylistic association, often summarised in a formal vocabulary, eg 'Rococo', 'Chinoiserie', 'Neo-classical'. These terms succinctly convey the affinity of the object with the social climate and fashion in which it circulated.

THE STATEMENT OF ORIGIN　　　　　　　　　　[Section　1.4.0]
The Statement of Origin is the most fundamental statement relating to a museum object, providing (as it does) particulars of that object's creation by human agency. For objects of natural origin (more usually called specimens) the Discovery Statement is more appropriate. The sources of our information on the origin of an object are so various that the terms in which it is expressed may be incomplete, approximate or detailed and exact. The cataloguer sometimes has a documentary source

111

(which may be referenced as a Citation in Section 3.4.0) but often has only an oral source, when details of origin and other historical aspects are received in conversation with the donor.

For many manufactured articles, the data on origin are derived from maker's marks on the object and from research into the whole range of his products. Where maker's marks are used it is necessary to extract relevant data and to present it in accordance with conventions devised for this Statement, but in addition to give a visual description of those marks in the Element reserved for that purpose (2.3.7). The Statement of Origin includes five Elements:

1.4.1   Firstly, we must answer the question "Who authorised, designed, produced or created the item?". This demands the name of a person or company. An individual's name may be that of a craftsman or artist; a company's name will usually suffice for objects produced by industry.

1.4.2   The maker's name is supplemented by a second Element defining maker's role, ie his/her contribution to the creation of the object. A limited number of options is available and these should be standardised by definition in a lexicon to avoid ambiguity. Suitable vocabulary includes 'artist', 'craftsman', 'designer', 'manufacturer' and (less obviously) 'taxidermist', the craftsman involved in preparing an animal exhibit. For coinage, the 'issuing authority' is logically seen as a role connected with the origin of the currency additional to that of 'moneyer': therefore, it belongs in this Element while the name of the authority itself occurs in Element (1.4.1). Two or more entries are made, if required, to record both the designer and the manufacturer of any object.

1.4.3   The process used in production should be described by a single term drawn from a list of standard descriptors applied within strict definitions. This Element plays a pre-eminent role in indexing and also in classifying many types of collections. For example, the word 'painting' entered here describes (and effectively classifies) every work of art created by that method. Other options available here include 'drawing', 'engraving', 'printing', 'casting', 'pressing', 'carving', etc.

1.4.4   The address Element contains information on the place at which the object was created or where the artist or craftsman resided. It may contain the full location or address of a private residence, studio or factory; or merely the name of a town or village.

1.4.5   This Element, called 'date of origin', is intended to be used only for a specific date, when definite information particular to the object is known with confidence. It must include a year date at least. When the date of origin is surmised, even by an acknowledged authority, it must be stated as a range of no more than five years to admit of entry here, eg 1825-29. Where exactitude or certainty are less than defined by these conditions, no date should be entered in this Section. Preferably information pertaining to the period of origin in broader terms, eg as decade, or quarter-century, should be treated as Classification by Age, and therefore should be entered in Section 2.2.0.

THE STATEMENT OF DERIVATION   [Section   1.5.0]
A work of art or craftsmanship is not infrequently modelled on a pre-viously existing object or image and it is helpful in understanding the subsequent work to know what artistic source it derives from. The relationship between the derived work and its precursor may be any-thing from thematic inspiration to plagiarism. The purpose of this Statement is to record significant facts about the precursor object that motivated the creator of the object under review. The following two examples illustrate contrasting situations in which this Statement can be applied:

The Spode plate (Example 25) reproduces a pictorial design which is derived from the combination of features from two aquatints, "Ponte Molle" and "The Gate of San Sebastian". Its sources are therefore recognisable, although it is itself an innovative work.

The Zoffoli bronze sculpture (Example 23) is "a reduction of the classical group on the Capitol (at) Rome: the base follows that designed by Michelangelo for the full-sized group" and thus it is a replica on a reduced scale, ie a skillful copy. The use of the Derivation Statement accentuates the fact that in this piece we have an example in miniature of Michelangelo's work. This sculpture can therefore be indexed by the

113

name of the classical sculptor as well as by the name of Zoffoli. In a similar way, the influence of the artist J Merigot on Spode's "Castle" design will be recognised in the relevant Statement of Derivation. The actual Elements to be considered under Derivation are:

1.5.1　　What object was the source of the artist's inspiration?

1.5.2　　Where is or was that source located?

1.5.3　　Who was the creator of that earlier work?

1.5.4　　When was that work itself created?

The freedom to express Derivation as a narrative statement must be defended where complexities and shades of meaning would otherwise be lost. For example, consider a drawing titled "Ariccia" attributed to Thomas Girtin. To explain its derivation we need to say, "This drawing is a close copy of J.R. Cozens' Ariccia and the assumption is that it should be regarded as one of the Monro School Copies". This sentence answers the question "What object was the source ..?" and therefore it must be entered in its entirety in Element 1.5.1. Additionally, the name "Cozens, J R" must be entered in Element 1.5.3 (maker's name) and this serves to index that reference.

THE DISCOVERY STATEMENT　　　　　　　　　　[Section　　1.6.0]

All objects of natural origin should have data to be recorded in this Section. Additionally those products of human craft and industry which were found in the environment in which they were used (or traded) are often accompanied by information about their discovery. Take care to exclude reference to objects that were "found" in the possession of any known person, in which case see Section 1.3.0 [Association].

　　　1.6.1　　The first Element requires the personal name of the finder. This Element may include a number of persons who acted in different capacities but were somehow instrumental in taking the object into a collection.

　　　1.6.2　　The second Element describes the role in which the said person acted, eg 'collector', 'excavator'. It is quite possible for a specimen to be procured by the actions of one person acting on the instructions of another, or as an aide to the collector, eg a 'trapper' working for a zoologist, and both require mention in this Element.

114

1.6.3   The date of the find (discovery, excavation, or capture from the wild) is an important piece of information to be stated precisely and at least a known year must be given. In the case of plants and animal specimens, the month is usually a significant component of the date because it signifies seasonal factors relating to flowering, fruiting, migration, breeding, moulting, etc.

1.6.4   The place of discovery or capture is of pre-eminent importance for the record of all natural specimens and for archaeological objects too. The words used to identify the place where the specimen occurred should be in the form of statement in which it is desired to print the information in any subsequent reports. As a minimum, it must include the name of a territory or settlement which is widely recognised and can be confirmed in the gazetteer of a world atlas. In most cases it will also contain a site name for the more exact locality. Attention should be given to creating a structured record of geographic position in the Section on Classification by Area [Section 2.2.0].

1.6.5   This Element is to record geographical co-ordinates, either as a national grid reference (up to 2 alphabetic and 6 numeric characters) or by latitude and longitude, to the nearest degree.

1.6.6   An Element called 'environment of discovery' is provided to record information of a descriptive kind relating to the immediate context in which the find or fragment (in archaeology) or specimen (in natural sciences) occurred. Its purpose is to identify the habitat of the living specimen and the lithology of the rock matrix in which the geological specimen was embedded. For an archaeological find we can record the exact position of the object in situ or the nature of the matrix directly surrounding it. Rock-units have regional or local names and these are appropriate to describe geological context, as also are the names of facies and fossil assemblage zones. In practice this Element serves as a stratigraphic index to records and specimens (cf 2.2.6).

1.6.7   This records the altitude above or below sea-level of the find-spot as an important adjunct to the geographical co-ordinates.

1.6.8   This Element is for on-site vertical measurements such as height above ground surface (or depth below it) or water-depth in environments such as lakes and rock-pools.

115

1.6.9   This provides for recording on-site horizontal measurements (co-ordinates) relating to a locally established grid, commonly employed in excavation work on historical and archaeological sites and in ecological surveys.

THE FUNCTION STATEMENT   [Section   1.7.0]

The function of an object can be considered both in a particular sense and in relation to broader social and economic activities. In some disciplines, eg ethnography, local history and technology, there is a strong emphasis on the functional characteristics of objects as an aid to classification (R.G. Chenhall, 1978; B. Blackwood, 1970). The first three Elements of this Section can be used for any three levels of the nomenclature in a hierarchic structure such as the SHIC classification. Additionally, the last Element may be reserved for a numeric code. The general definition of the components of this Section now follows:

1.7.1   In what trade, industry, craft or context was the object used? This is, in effect, the broad term of a functional classification if strict hierarchy is employed or if free choice is allowed in the addition of names it provides an index to those aspects of an object's utility; eg 'Ritual Objects' in the Pitt Rivers Classification (Blackwood, 1970).

1.7.2   In what process or activity was the object used?

1.7.3   What was its precise function, ie the effect of its use?

1.7.4   How was it operated? or How did it function?

The information that can be accepted in Element 1.7.4 may refer to the manner in which the implement or machine was powered, eg 'manually' or 'steam-driven' and in that case it demands concise data. In other cases, it may involve a narrative explanation of how the article was manipulated or applied to the task for which it was designed.

1.7.5   In what circumstances was the object used? This Element relates less to technical equipment used in craft or industry than to articles of ceremonial, ritual, and other event-oriented functions. It can be expressed either at length in free text or in more concise form according to any appropriate convention, eg 'Hunting Ritual'.

1.7.6   Where was the object used /in operation? This Element accepts data of a specific kind describing the actual location. (cf 1.3.3)

116

1.7.7   When was the object used /in operation? (See also 1.3.4.)

1.7.8   Who was the user of this object when it was in operation or performing its function?   Care is necessary not to duplicate data given in Element 1.3.1.

These three Elements (above) have an essential role in collections where functional aspects tend to be dominant features of the record, in comparison with collections in which information on the objects' actual use is incidental and of erratic occurrence.   In the latter situation, if an object is known in use only on a single occasion, it may be more appropriate to regard the incident as 'association' by place, event or date (not as 'function') and therefore enter the data in Section 1.3.0.

1.7.9   This final Element is reserved for a numeric classification either by function or by operational context, such as that provided by the Social History and Industrial Classification (SHIC, 1983).

———————

Chapter 8
Descriptive data

This chapter explains the composition of the Second-Tier Sections of the reference framework REFORM. The common feature of these Sections, is that the included Statements comprise information of a static character concerned with describing the physical features of objects and (like First-Tier Statements) they provide the permanent core of every record. These salient facts about an object do not change but opportunity is needed to amend data as and when it is found to be inexact or capable of improvement.

The Statements are examined in sequence beginning with the most immediate, the Statement of the object's Identity, and then proceeds through Classification to the recording of Description, Maker's Marks, Inscription and Imagery. Each of the Statements is structured by division into a number of Elements, some of which are formal, being designed for data that is defined in its presentation as well as content, while others can be used for expressions of variable length which may be subject to conventions of syntax to facilitate indexing by keyword.

THE IDENTITY STATEMENT   [Section 2.1.0]
The Identity Statement is the pivotal component of the individual record about an object and it is fundamental to the process of registration. It contains all those Elements which establish the unique identity of the

individual object and which distinguish it from all others (even those of the same type and origin). Some of the identifying attributes specific to an object are artificial devices such as its manufacturer's serial number and the accession number allocated to it by the museum. Others include references to photographs and drawings of the object which visually record its individuality.

2.1.1   The first Element, of absolute importance, is Accession Number, without which an object cannot be recorded (except as an Inward Loan, for which see Section 4.4.0). The precise form in which the Accession Number is presented is defined in accordance with strict conventions by each museum but the principle can be stated that it consists always of sequential numbers, alphabetic characters and/or punctuation. Its exact form must be completely standardised so that records for every object may be consistently listed and retrieved by computer. Accession Number can be entered only once and duplicates are obviously invalid. When an object is de-requisitioned by reason of loss or disposal, this relatively rare event is recorded in Section 4.1.0 as a change of Status.

2.1.2   Code letters (or an abbreviation) for the name of the department in which the object has been deposited provide an infallible method of segregating records by department for convenience in printed listings.

2.1.3   It is desirable to include the registration date on which the record was made. In retrospect this can assume some importance, for example, when a large private collection is received containing several hundreds of objects: registering individual items is then an extended process, continuing long after the collection was received (see Element 1.1.7).

2.1.4   If the individual object has a title, as usual in the case of pictorial representations, this Element enables it to be recorded. Thought must be given to the purposes for which this information will ultimately be needed. If it is to be available solely for reporting, (ie reiteration on demand) natural expression of the title, word by word, will be preferred. On the other hand, if it will be incorporated in lists of titles and if these have to be sorted and presented in alphabetic

119

sequence, then consideration should be given to modifying the actual order of words because the first word of the title obviously determines its position in the list.

In the case of manufactured objects, particularly those which are now described as 'consumer goods', there is often a name given to the design, model or series of a product which (although it is not unique to the individual) fulfills the same role as the title of an artistic work. For example, a style or pattern of textile fabric may have a name and a production series of bicycles has a referable identity when given a title such as "Roadmaster". It can be useful to select items by designations of this kind and both retrieval and listing are aided by this Element.

In cataloguing coins, this Element covers the denomination or face value, which is (in a special sense) a series name or title, whether it be 'doubloon', 'guinea' or '5 cent piece'.

2.1.5   The purpose of having an Element containing a Brief Description is explained by the discussion of naming things in Chapter 1. Names are actually classificatory terms, so they are not found here as adjuncts to Identity but occur as Elements of Classification in Section 2.2.0. The name given to an object is insufficient to identify the individual item without the support of an expanded description, which is the principal concern of Section 2.3.0. However, on registering an object it is necessary to characterise it in the space of a brief sentence and this Element is intended to meet that requirement. Its prime purpose is to recall the essential and individual characteristics of the object so as to facilitate its recognition, eg "Candlesticks, a pair, bronze, Italian; with baluster-shaped stem and flat base supported on four feet". It also meets a practical necessity as a concise 'aide memoire' to relate constituent parts of composite objects, eg "300Kv Van Der Graaf generator c/w particle accelerator, associated vacuum equipment, magnet and 5 racks of control electronics".

Brief Description may be freely constructed in any way that serves its purpose: there need be no prohibition on including some data which recur as separate Elements elsewhere within the record. In this regard it is exceptional and breaks a rule that governs all other Elements because it is omnivalent. If, as is strongly advised, Brief Description

120

is limited absolutely to not more than two lines in length, it can be extremely useful for inclusion in many types of report (see Chapter 11).

2.1.6   The name of the curator responsible for originating the record and for its accuracy is indispensible to a system in which the source of all data is ideally traceable. The insertion of a person's name in this Element also serves to record the identifier and classifier of the item.

2.1.7   If the object carries any pre-existing identity number (eg if it was received from a large private collection) that number is separately recorded here. For archaeological artefacts this would be the correct place to include the excavator's number because it too is a unique reference to the object's identity. For manufactured products there is usually a Serial Number marked on the object itself, perhaps on various parts or else assigned to the whole assembly as a single unit, eg "Rolls-Royce Conway jet engine Mk.540, Serial No.7031". In this case the name given to the Model or Series (Element 2.1.4) is "Conway, Mk 540" while the Serial Number unique to this example of the engine is 7031 (Element 2.1.7).

2.1.8   Recognising the practical value of a photographic record for many types of museum object, the purpose of this Element is to register the existence of negatives and/or transparencies (distinguished by prefix) and to cite their reference numbers.

2.1.9   The last Element of the Identity Statement makes similar provision for reference to museum drawings which may serve as further aids to identification, for example: profile drawings of archaeological sherds.

THE CLASSIFICATION SECTION   [Section   2.2.0]

The placement of Classification next in importance to Identity is intentional, although many would expect Description to take precedence. Indeed, by elevating Classification to the status of a Section, REFORM focusses the attention of curators and cataloguers on the vital role that classification performs. In doing so, it compels them to think about the position of every object received in relation to the totality of the collection, and to do this at an early stage in the cataloguing process.

Classified terms provide anchor-points which tie the newly-received object into established collections. In classifying every object by one or more of these criteria, the cataloguer labels the record with terms that assign the object to membership of various groups. This is not an academic exercise: in fact it has great practical significance, recognising that the ultimate purpose of classification is to enable searches to be made to retrieve records according to predetermined criteria.

The effect of each classificatory Element, of course, is to assign every object to 'a group' but if more than one classificatory criterion is stipulated each item can belong to more than one group. For example

group 1:	forks	silver	18th century
group 2:	English	silver	18th century
group 3:	English	cutlery	George II

(the same object as a member of three differently constituted groups). The classified profile of any item can be subtly refined in REFORM by combining classifications which are not mutually exclusive, eg historic, geographic and typological, each of them having a 3-level hierarchy. In addition, some of the Elements included in several other Sections are classificatory in effect: substance in Section 2.3.0, functional attributes in Section 1.7.0 and association by context in Section 1.3.0. Optionally, each object can be classified by age, by region, by type, by function and by context, selecting one or more of these as appropriate. While most objects can be assigned to a period and to an area of origin, some of the remaining methods of classification are relevant only to certain kinds of collections: thus, functional classification (1.7.0) is required for Folk-Life objects but irrelevant for Paintings. Indeed, Paintings can be better classified by medium (2.3.3) and by aspects of Imagery such as subject (Section 2.6.0) rather than by object-type as such. For classifications that are admittedly mixed, depending on object-type at one level and on function or substance at another level, these varied Elements may be used in suitable combination in a computerised system.

Geographic Classification

It is not inherently a purpose of REFORM to prescribe which system of classification should be used but rather to produce examples illustrating the method of working envisaged. It is useful to recognise the possibility of treating the three Elements of this Statement on a sliding scale against divisions of area. Museums whose collections are entirely local can use these Elements for names of county, parish and landed estate, ignoring the global and national levels completely. In contrast, those with world-wide collections may prefer to adopt the range of global and territorial divisions outlined below. There is some risk of duplicating data which appears under Origin [Element 1.4.4] or under Discovery [Element 1.6.4] but these provide full information for purposes of report while the classified Elements [this Section] are for analysing and relating records by geography.

2.2.1   The first and broadest Element of geographical classification is the GEO-CODE. In subjects such as Archaeology, Ethnography and Natural History it is obviously useful to classify collected material by global divisions. An appropriate scheme to achieve this needs a framework of strict geometry, as provided by lines of latitude and longitude, to establish unambiguous boundaries between major world zones. Not only must it demarcate the continental land-masses but all islands must be capable of reference, as also must oceanic areas. It remains then to ensure that those countries and islands that are related by their ethnic culture or by natural affinities of climate, flora, and fauna are not artificially segregated by the zonal boundaries.

As a result of thorough geographical appraisal it is found that the demarcation of global divisions can be made along the following lines:

a)   from North Pole along meridian of longitude 30°W

b)   from North Pole along meridian of longitude 60°E

c)   a latitudinal division along the parallel of latitude 20°N

d)   a latitudinal division along the parallel of latitude 10°S

e)   in the Pacific sector, above latitude 20°N, a N-S division along meridian 180°

f)   in the Pacific sector, below lat.20°N and above lat.60°S, two divisions on meridians of 155°E and 120°W

g)   a latitudinal division along the parallel 60°S.

When plotted, these boundaries divide the world into twelve zones. Each global zone can be conveniently referenced by an alphabetic code of four characters (called a GEO-CODE) which is mnemonic.   Thus:

EQAM = equatorial belt, American sector

EQAF = equatorial belt, African sector

EQAS = equatorial belt, Asiatic sector

EQPA = equatorial belt, Pacific sector

SOAM = southern belt, American sector

SOAF = southern belt, African sector

SOAU = southern belt, Australian sector

SOPA = southern belt, Pacific sector

NOAM = northern belt, American sector

PALW = western Palearctic (Europe,N.Africa,Middle East)

PALE = eastern Palearctic (northern Asia)

ANTA = Antarctica

The Geocode can be usefully augmented by adding a two-letter suffix to identify the individual country being referenced, using the first two letters of the name of the country for this purpose. The result is a 6-letter code, eg PALEJA (= Japan), which uniquely identifies each country (and major island or group of islands) and also places it within a global quadrangle which enables continental groups to be recognised. When interpreted by computer, these codes provide a powerful indexing tool, making it possible to formulate enquiries as broadly or narrowly as the purpose requires. The first two letters alone define the major latitudinal belts of the world.

2.2.2   The second Element is the name of a country, either as defined by national frontiers (ie a political state) or as the name of an island which may or may not coincide with the frontiers of a nation-state. For example, New Guinea is an island comprising two distinct national territories but it is an unambiguous geographic unit, similarly in the case of Borneo. In other cases islands are significant natural units even when they form part of larger nations, eg Java, Sumatra (parts of Indonesia), and they should be always recognised as countries in their own right.

124

2.2.3   The third Element is the name of a province within a country (or within an island regarded as being a 'country'). These may be cultural regions and not necessarily administrative divisions: the actual area of territory denoted varies.   Where the national territory is very large, eg United States of America, the 'province' will be the name of a single state, eg Wisconsin, but if the nation or island is small, eg the United Kingdom, the 'province' will be the individual county.   More precise details of locality are given in the Statement of Origin [Section 1.4.0] or in the Discovery Statement [Section 1.6.0] as appropriate.

Classification by Age

The age of individual museum objects is in many instances one of the most interesting and informative facts contributing to the significance of its visible features.   It is reasonable therefore to attempt to classify an object by its age and so relate it to a host of others and to the period in which it was made.

2.2.4   The first Element of temporal classification offers the broadest possible divisions of time, using the names accorded within disciplines to the most general levels of culture and technology in a time context.   For example, here we find names like Iron Age, Neolithic, Mediaeval.

2.2.5   The second Element accepts names of dynasties, royal houses and individual monarchs, where these terms are regarded as assignments to specific periods of time with terminal dates that are clearly understood; for example, Regency, William & Mary, Georgian. These terms should not be used loosely, eg where there is doubt on authenticity or the correctness of the dating implied.   Purely stylistic inferences, lacking sure foundation of date, are better reported in Association [Element 1.3.7].

2.2.6   Year of manufacture, or else of origin, is an Element in the Statement of Origin [Element 1.4.5], so it is not necessary to repeat it in the Classification by Age.   A broader perspective of time is required here, in which an object is assigned to a period as defined in numerical terms and in which intervals are of equal length.   Normally a century should be specified and optionally, perhaps a quarter-century,

125

eg 17th century (1st quarter). This is suitable for classifying objects of historical date but for prehistoric materials such as those studied and dated by archaeological methods, 'millenium' is a more appropriate unit in place of 'century', eg 3rd millenium BC (4th quarter).

The three-part historical classification outlined above allows those Elements to be used which most closely match the degree of precision attached to dating of an object. It is not necessary to classify an object under all three Time Elements (indeed that is unlikely) but that choice remains open.

In the special case of geological records, the three age classes are used quite differently to accommodate names of chronological units from the geological time-scale but not names of stratigraphic units or litho-logical terms, which should be entered under 'environment of discovery' (Element 1.6.6). Usually it will be convenient to include the names of geological period, series, and stage /sub-stage (Odin, 1982), as in the example: Carboniferous; Upper; Westphalian;

Classification by Type Function and Context

Traditional museum schemes of classification have been characterised as "classifications of convenience" (M A Vanns, 1984) which is to say they are founded on pragmatic considerations rather than theoretical grounds. Categories that are used to subdivide major groups tend to be chosen for their immediate practicality when applied to a particular collection (which may be unbalanced in its representation): we have seen enough examples of this in Chapters 1 to 3. Criteria that serve as the basis for subdivision in one series may be abandoned and replaced by quite different criteria in another series of objects in the same main group. This generates what can only be called mixed classifications.

However, looking at such schemes with a degree of detachment, it is possible to distinguish three principal criteria that are commonly involved and of which any one can be treated independently of the others. These classificatory criteria are form, function and context. It does require a conscious mental effort to dissociate terms based on functional attributes from those based on aspects of typology, such as constructional features, morphology and characteristic forms of design

126

and embellishment. Nevertheless, it is advantageous to apply this distinction because it increases the number of classified terms that are then available for sorting, grouping and retrieval.

Under the provisions of REFORM, it is intended to allow any object to be classified in each of these modes: by type, function and context. This Section includes Classification by Type while function is treated in Section 1.7.0 and context in Section 1.3.0. Rarely is it necessary to utilize all of these classificatory Elements: instead, the most relevant can be chosen to suit retrieval requirements for a particular collection.

Typological Classification

Avoiding nomenclature involving assignment by function and context (not so easy as it seems), most schemes of object names can be arranged into a three-tier hierarchy of types. Attributes of morphology can be included in type names but materials should not be involved in the naming of types because materials are recognised separately under Element 2.3.3 and this can be invoked when required. Some collections can be classified by adopting a generally recognised scheme which is regarded as authoritative, such as the ICOM Classification for Costume, while in others a suitable scheme may have to be assembled to reflect the special composition of the collection.

Three Elements are allocated to typological classification and these form a series comparable with the threefold division of geographic and time concepts.

2.2.7   This is the highest level of hierarchic nomenclature for object type and therefore accepts the broad term in any series of three levels, generally a major class name.

2.2.8   This is the intermediate level of hierarchic nomenclature for object type and therefore accepts the middle term in any three-part series of names, often a sub-class name.

2.2.9   This Element is for the lowest level of classified name (whether the preceding two Elements are entered or not) and usually it records the common (group-) name for a type of object, eg flute, frock, sword, table, watch, etc. Unless a lexicon of preferred terms is created, when not using an established classification, there is a risk of proliferating synonyms and related terms, so proceed with caution! Any term that describes the object more specifically, without imposing vocabulary control, should be included in the Brief Description (2.1.5).

In classifying specimens of plants, animals and their fossilised remains, curators of biological and palaeontological collections have recourse to the binomial system of nomenclature founded by Linnaeus. This situation is thoroughly familiar to curators in those disciplines but for others it should be mentioned that in natural sciences the classification itself becomes the system of naming. For these subjects the idea of a 'simple name' is less important, if not actually redundant, and serves only to record the so-called 'common name' given in English. Under REFORM these common names can be used as the leading term in the Brief Description (Element 2.1.5).

For specimens in natural sciences, as for any other object, we use the three Elements of the Typological Classification and equate them to appropriate levels in a taxonomic hierarchy. Usually the Latin binomial (complete with its authors name) is regarded as the narrow term and is treated as one Element (2.2.9), Family name becomes the middle term (2.2.8) and the natural Order comprises the broad term (2.2.7).

Many cataloguers recognise that it is not essential to include classified nomenclature at every level because a numerical code, such as the Universal Decimal Classification, can perform equivalent functions for retrieval purposes. In social sciences a similar role is performed by the Social History and Industrial Classification, which provides codes of numerical form for extensive subdivision of human activities. For mineral substances, including gemstones, a three-part classification is in general use (Hey, 1955) which is indexed by a numerical code that uniquely references each mineral variety. The simplest way to employ this is to cite the reference number in Element 2.2.7. The broad term of Hey's classification is probably not very meaningful to non-specialists (class names such as 'alumino-silicates', 'antimonites' etc) but the medial term identifies the metals present in each mineral (silver, titanium, zinc etc) and this may well be worthy of record in Element 2.2.8. Names of particular mineral species (for which Hey gives synonyms) serve as the narrow term of his classification: these logically occupy Element 2.2.9.

The description of an object is at the very core of any record relating to it. Because the REFORM Information System is designed to fulfill both administrative and curatorial functions, separate provision is made for describing each item in relation to the Catalogues and the Register. For registration purposes and for convenience in the production of lists there is an Element called Brief Description [2.1.5] in the Statement of Identity.   In contrast to the conciseness of that Element, which is ideal for managerial requirements, catalogues contain a full Descriptive Statement which includes several data Elements.   These are important facets of descriptive information which ideally should be separable so that any of them may be extracted for listing with related data about the objects. To explain this section of REFORM in use, we take as an example the description of an ethnographic item of earthenware:

Example 33   Ethnography
                Pottery, bichrome ware, jug.
   [Brief Description]
                Globular jug with tapered neck, buff slip, painted
                        in black and red.
   [Text Description]
                °Ring-base°, globular body, medium tapered °neck° with
                ridge at junction with °handle°, pinched rim, curved
                handle from half-way up neck to shoulder. On each side,
                concentric °design° of black °lines° and °bands° and on
                shoulder °pattern° of vertical black lines and °chequer-
                board° design, flanked on each side by °quadrants° of
                black and red °concentric° lines.   Below handle, a group
                of black concentric °circles° enclosed by black circular
                band. On front, design of black concentric semi-circles,
                concentric °triangles° in black and red, concentric quad-
                rants of red and black lines and black horizontal lines.
                On the neck, black lines and bands with one band of
                °zigzag° °decoration°.   Handle with black line down each
                edge with joining horizontal lines between.

129

In the preceding Text Description there are obviously some words that characterise the vessel and these same words would be extremely useful in finding other vessels with more or less similar features. These are the 'keywords' but here, in an Element of unlimited length, they are dispersed throughout the paragraph: there is no way to isolate them without resorting to fragmentation of the narrative. By selecting only those terms that might be included in a search request, 14 words have been marked with the superscript symbol °, as prefix and suffix. Assuming that this symbol (or another substituted in its place) can be used as a sign of demarcation (known as a delimiter) in the computer program of our choice, these terms can be incorporated automatically into an 'inverted file'* to aid their rapid retrieval. In the absence of this special facility they can be retrieved by 'free-text search'*. (* computing techniques are discussed in Chapter 12).

2.3.1   The Element called Text Description allows the cataloguer to record in connected prose those attributes that are not adequately expressed by other Elements of this Section but it should not duplicate them. With reference to Example 33, this allows us to record details of surface decoration represented by 14 keywords while Element 2.3.5 may be used to summarise Decoration in a single term (eg 'geometric'). Text Description can be used to expand on any aspect of an object that is available to inspection and is not treated elsewhere, such as mention of constructional details, eg "corners of drawers dovetailed" or "base of cabinet has a false floor with compartment beneath".

While reviewing the versatile and accommmodating features of the REFORM record structure, it is instructive to compare the treatment of Example 33 with the style in which the same record is handled under a system developed in England by the Museum Documentation Association. Terms in square brackets are names of Elements; round brackets are used to enclose 'detail' (in the MDA sense, meaning not a keyword).

Simple Name: Jug
[Materials]   Pottery
    [Part]   [Aspect]   [Description]
    Base :   shape   :ring
    Body: shape   :globular

Neck :   shape   :tapered (ridge at junction with handle)

Rim :   shape   :pinched

Handle: position   :(from halfway up neck to shoulder)

The MDA view is that "it will be desirable to make ... these statements as brief as possible". The MDA Handbook states, "this section is not suitable for very detailed descriptive data ...". The best that could be done under MDA rules is to add another sequence of equally fragmented data, one set for each part of the jug, for example:

[Part]   [Aspect]   [Description]

Body: decoration: lines & bands (black)

Shoulder: decoration: lines & chequerboard (black)

Side :   decoration: quadrants & concentric (black red)

Front :   decoration: semi-circles & concentric & triangles
                          & quadrants & lines

Neck :   decoration: lines & bands & zigzag

Handle: decoration: line (down each edge) &
                          horizontal (joining lines)

Fragmentation of this kind causes complete dismemberment of natural language with the consequent loss of relational and holistic meaning. In this form, data can only be perceived as a listing of fragments which makes no sense as a whole. Contrast with this treatment the rather different option called 'segmentation' offered by REFORM. If we wish to avoid including any paragraph as long as the Text Description from Example 33, there is an alternative using a data Element called 'Part'.

2.3.2   This Element allows individual parts of an object to be named and described. On this basis, the same record appears in the following form. The Element is repeated as many times as necessary, once for each part, indicated by letters (a-f); index terms underlined:

a> <u>Sides</u>, concentric design of black lines and bands;

b> <u>Shoulder</u>, pattern of vertical black lines and chequerboard design; flanked on each side by quadrants of black /red concentric lines.

c> <u>Front</u>, design of black concentric semi-circles, concentric triangles in black and red, concentric quadrants of red and black lines, and black horizontal lines.

d> <u>Handle</u> with black line down each edge and joining horizontal lines;

131

e> <u>Handle</u> (below) group of black concentric circles surrounded by black circular band.

f> <u>Neck</u>, black lines and bands with one band of zigzag decoration.

By this treatment each part-description can be isolated if desired and retrieved independently of the others. This manoeuvre is not possible when the combined data are treated as a single paragraph.

In addition to Text Description and Part (which is optional in use) the Section includes the following Elements to accommodate particulars of descriptive information, illustrated by reference to Example 33.

Element: 2.3.3 = Substance <u>earthenware</u>,

2.3.4 = Form <u>globular</u> with tapering neck

2.3.5 = Decoration <u>geometric</u>

All of the terms underlined are intended for indexing and retrieval. These three Elements are intended to be classificatory and therefore imply the use of controlled vocabulary or even a vocabulary limited to a finite number of options (determinate vocabulary). In other Elements we accept data that may be infinitely varied, eg Measurement.

2.3.3   'Substance' is a descriptive Element that is indispensable in records for objects of every kind and is commonly employed as a major attribute for purposes of indexing and classification: alternatively it is called 'Material'. The form in which information is recorded under this Element must be designed to meet the requirements for retrieval. Free-text is inadvisable here because it can only be retrieved by association with the record identifier and is not suitable for listing, eg (of a bicycle) "constructed from Reynolds 531 tube throughout".

Man-made objects commonly include several different substances in their various parts, so one option is to state the principal material here and record others in the description of the respective parts [2.3.2]. Alternatively, all constituent substances may be listed in Element 2.3.3 in descending order of importance.

With reference to paintings and drawings, the record of Substance is treated as referring to the medium and its supporting fabric, eg 'watercolour on paper', 'oil on canvas', 'black ink on board', 'tempera on wood panel', etc. The materials of the frame and /or mount are conveniently treated under the separate Element called Part.

132

With reference to geological specimens, both fossils and minerals, this Element records the Substance of which the specimen is formed and therefore, very usefully allows the chemical name to be stated and indexed. For fossil material, the mineral of which it is composed can be substituted if preferred, eg 'calcite' or 'calcium carbonate'. For mineral ores, the mineral name is used as the classified name [2.2.9] and the 'Substance' Element is used to record chemical composition; eg for the mineral 'galena', we may record Substance = 'lead sulphide'.

2.3.4   This Element is reserved for descriptors of shape or 'Form'. It can be used for free text if the appearance of an object demands unique description, eg "conical with small knob at the top, like a modern chess pawn". Where the form that is characteristic for the type of object is well known, this Element can be used to note only those features of shape peculiar to the individual example /specimen, ie those which deviate from the norm.

Commonly, however, 'Form' employs a lexicon of strictly defined terms and optionally it can be structured to contain just two or three of these. For example, where a series of similar objects can be separated more precisely by features of their shape, the use of appropriate terms can show degrees of likeness and degrees of difference between any sets that may be selected, as in the following series of arrow-heads.

> triangular, acute tip, truncate base
> triangular, asymmetric, truncate base
> triangular, acute tip, tanged base
> lobate, waisted, truncate base
> lobate, serrate edge, tanged base

Comparability is aided by observing a convention for syntax, such that the term for an object's general (overall) shape precedes any qualifying descriptor and descriptors for its apex and base, in that order. With reference to geological specimens, the special function of this Element is to describe in standard terminology the solid geometrical form developed in crystalline minerals, eg 'monoclinal'.

2.3.5   This Element, to describe 'Surface Decoration', can be treated in any way comparable with the choice elaborated for 'Form'. Probably it is best employed with a controlled vocabulary but otherwise it may be treated either at length or, depending on retrieval requirements for the record, as a summary category relating to particulars given elsewhere under Text Description or Part Description. It then serves as an index (or classification) of superficial decorative features.

For biological specimens, this is the appropriate Element in which to record all kinds of surface markings, eg on animal pelts, and the type and condition of plumage of birds, using a suitable determinate vocabulary to allow search and retrieval of similar states, eg 'winter plumage', 'breeding plumage', 'erythrytic variety', 'albino', etc.

2.3.6 Measurement of objects of symmetrical shape, whether on a circular or rectangular base, is defined by height and diameter or by height, length and width respectively. The use of measures other than size, such as weight, must also be facilitated. At least four dimensions may therefore be needed in any record and to these must be added others peculiar to objects of irregular shape. Consequently a 'measurement' Element can be repeated as many times as needed to cover all aspects of the object that are measured. Some examples are:

"diameter of base 24 cm" ;   "diameter (maximum) 34 cm" ;

"height to shoulder 81 cm" ;   "weight without lid 180 gm" ;

Each repeat of this Element includes three components: dimension, value (ie numerical quantity measured) and units in which it was measured.

2.3.7 Natural history specimens (of animals especially) are normally distinguished by gender (male or female), this being a major characteristic of descriptive importance. The same distinction is also usually made in reference to garments of clothing in costume collections according to the sex of the wearer. Additionally, in both contexts, it is necessary to describe the life-stage of the individual, not in years but in terms of development or maturity, eg in the human example by terms such as 'infant', 'child', 'youth', 'adult'. For animals there are special terms relating to each natural group, eg 'larva', 'pupa', 'imago' (insects); 'egg', 'nestling', 'juvenile', 'immature' and 'adult' (birds).

MAKER'S MARK STATEMENT   [Section   2.4.0]
The Description Statement records the physical form and structural details but many objects also display markings as text or symbols that

indicate authorship or authenticity, either overtly or in cryptic form. These are the subject of statements in this Section, which are regarded as being quite distinct from 'inscriptions' [Section 2.5.0]. If there are several marks of different kinds on the object there must be a clear and separate Statement for each one of them, including the constituent Elements described in the following paragraphs.

For works of art, Maker's Marks are represented by the artist's signature or personal emblem (eg Whistler's butterfly motif) together with ancillary marks, such as date or place, written by the originator. However, if the artist also wrote a phrase of dedication on the work, this is treated as an Inscription: the details to be recorded are closely comparable but the Statement of Inscription is filed separately [2.5.0].

For works of manufactured origin, Marks have an important role in aiding recognition of the series, model or date of the manufactured article. These data are not always explicit but frequently the design of the maker's trademark establishes the period of years in which the article was produced, eg porcelain marks, silver hallmarks.

2.4.1   The first Element of the Mark Statement, therefore, defines the type of mark, using a determinate list of approved terms, eg signature, monogram, emblem, trademark, hallmark, assay mark, patent number, serial number. A suitable term, comparable with these, is needed for a type of mark in which the maker's (company) name and trade address are directly stated: for this purpose the term 'housemark' is proposed.

2.4.2   For every mark thus defined the second Element records where on the object the mark is found, eg "on the base, central".

2.4.3   Thirdly, the method used in making the mark is named, choosing an appropriate word for the process from a determinate list of terms, eg 'engraved', 'printed', 'stamped'. In the case of hand-marked wares the term 'scribed' is recommended, and reference to the medium may be appended, eg "scribed in ink"; "scribed in red chalk", etc.

2.4.4   The next Element is a transcript of the text of the mark itself or a description of the motif if it takes a symbolic form. In the latter case it is necessary to interpret the motif in terms of its significance and this is the purpose of the final Element in the Statement.

2.4.5   An explanatory phrase, for example, 'Sterling silver' or 'Britannia silver', is recorded to interpret the symbol used as a mark and, where a hallmark is shown, the year and name of the assay office is stated.

THE INSCRIPTION STATEMENT   [Section   2.5.0]

The Inscription Statement is to record all textual material excepting Maker's Marks.   Inscriptions are texts of dedication, commemoration, celebration, proclamation, eg to record an honour, a sentiment or even a commercial tract.   The most obvious examples are found in numismatic collections as the inscriptions on coins and medals: separate Statements are written for the texts on obverse and reverse sides.   With reference to pictures, a plaque bearing the title (a form of proclamation) is often affixed to the frame or, especially with prints, the title may appear beneath the image or on the mount; all of which qualify as inscriptions. Information given on labels affixed to any object can be treated similarly if it is accepted practice within the museum to record them.   Whatever the example, this Section provides opportunity to record written inform- ation that is visible on the object.   The Elements of an Inscription Statement are as follow:

2.5.1   Firstly an accurate transcription is made where the original text is in the Roman alphabet but not when it appears in any script which cannot be reproduced without special type-setting, eg Hebrew, Arabic, Cyrillic and the cuneiform characters of ancient Assyria (Example 7).

2.5.2   Secondly, inscriptions that are not written in the modern language of the cataloguing institution require translation into that language.   This translation supplements the literal transcript when the original is a contemporary foreign language, eg the German inscription on the prize-medal for music (Example 19).   Where the original is an archaic text in a dead language, translation takes on greater importance because the reader's comprehension depends entirely upon it. This is especially true if the original is in a script that cannot be reproduced, eg the cuneiform text from the Temple at Nineveh (Example 7).

2.5.3   The language in which the inscription appears should be stated. This Element of data is intended to facilitate rapid search and selection of records where choice of language is significant.

2.5.4   For such reasons, the method by which the inscription was made on the object is recorded, ('printed', 'stamped', 'engraved', 'scribed', etc) together with the medium used, if appropriate. This is informative not only in a technical sense but also because it indicates the visual properties of the inscription better than any other single descriptor.

2.5.5   Finally, the position of the inscription on the object must be stated. Note that it is possible to express this more precisely than often is achieved in practice. For example, with reference to the commemorative jug in praise of Wellington (Example 14), instead of reporting the position of the verse as "on one side", it could easily be improved by adding the phrase "with handle to right" (or 'left'): likewise for the verse celebrating the Boxer of Birmingham Town.

THE STATEMENT ON IMAGERY   [Section   2.6.0]

The subject matter of drawings, paintings, etchings and all forms of two-dimensional representation, whether illustrative or allegorical, is conceptually quite distinct from the physical description of pictures as objects, which corresponds to the physical description of every other kind of museum object.

The Description Statement [Section 2.3.0] records tangible features such as the size of the picture, the mount and lining, the medium and substrate, the frame and any labels or markings. Equivalent physical attributes exist in reference to other objects which may be vehicles for imagery, such as tapestries, stained-glass, plaques, etc. At this physical plane of description, the image could be recorded in terms of the distribution of pigments. In contrast to these external features, the representational content is interpretive, or even introspective. It is an expression of the artist's message, emotion, or perception (which of these depending on the character of the work) but in all cases it is distinct from the actual medium in which the image was made.

Hence, in REFORM a separate Section exists for representational aspects of the image. The Statement on Imagery includes Elements to analyse and record the subjects and things shown. Pictorial devices incorporated in or upon utilitarian objects such as ceramic wares, jewellery boxes, biscuit tins and tiles can be described as Decoration under the provisions of the Description Statement [Element 2.3.5] but when there is more than decorative significance in the illustration it can be treated as 'imagery' for a more detailed record.

One of the most compelling reasons for recording data in this Section is the desire to index pictorial material according to its subject. The organisation of this Section allows retrieval of those aspects of a picture which refer to a time context, to persons and social groups, to a multitude of objects, to topographic locations, and activities /events. It also enables sorting and listing of these topics to be effected. The way in which this is handled depends upon the facilities available in the computer software. As in other Sections, one option is to keep entries brief and to insist that each begins with the relevant keyword through which the data can be retrieved. One word of caution, it is neceeasry to distinguish data entered into this Section from that filed into the Classification Section [2.2.0]. To clarify this point, Classification of a picture by Age refers to the period when the work was executed, but data relating to the time Element given in this Section [Imagery] refers to the period depicted in the picture itself. Component Elements of this Section are the following.

2.6.1   The illustrative role of the image may be classified, eg as 'portrait', 'figure', 'landscape', 'seascape', etc. Here also we may indicate the artistic purpose of the work, for example, distinguishing 'devotional' (religious), 'historical' (eg depiction of battle scenes), 'literary', 'narrative', 'allegorical' and so on. Next come particulars of the subject analysed under several of the following Elements:

2.6.2   things depicted (including animals but not persons), eg rural scene, street scene, harbour and ships;

2.6.3   personages or groups of persons, eg Duke of Wellington or 'soldiers';

2.6.4   place, area or region illustrated (place-names may be suitable for indexing or can be expressed in narrative form for passive retrieval;

2.6.5   period depicted (may create a historical index if subject to observance of a lexicon of preferred terms);

2.6.6   activities or events shown, eg "loading cargo", "trooping the colour" or "bathing" (cf Beham woodcut; Example 24).

A quite different application of this Section is illustrated by the description of Imagery held on a reel of film catalogued by the Imperial War Museum (Smither, 1985). As with a static picture, the film's title, "Trial drops of the 'Kurt' bouncing bomb" belongs in the Title Element of the Identity Section [2.1.4]. The paragraph of unstructured text that follows is an Imagery Statement:

> "The bombs, both with and without attached rocket unit, are seen being released both singly and (in two cases) in pairs from a low-flying aircraft (FW 190). They bounce across the water for some distance before sinking and, in the final drop only, exploding. The drops are filmed from various camera positions both in slow motion and at normal speed. 'Aus Beton' in the title implies that all except the last bomb are concrete-filled test weapons."

Certain Elements of data can be extracted from this to create a normally structured record, eg:

2.6.1 (Illustrative ROLE of the Image): documentary

2.6.2 (THINGS depicted): bombs ; aircraft, FW 190; rocket unit;

2.6.5 (PERIOD depicted): World War 2

2.6.6 (EVENTS shown): weapon testing; bombs exploding;

Having extracted these components, certain information remains which has not been captured in the above Elements, eg camera speeds, 'aus Beton', mode of release, behaviour on water, etc and this suggests a need for the option of an additional Element (2.6.7) to accommodate narrative free-text comparable with that provided for textual material in the Description Statement.

REFERENCES

Blackwood, B. (1970) "The Classification of Artefacts in the Pitt Rivers Museum Oxford" University of Oxford, Pitt Rivers Museum. Occasional Papers in Technology, 11. 94pp.

Chenhall, R.G. (1978) "Nomenclature for Museum Cataloguing: a system for classifying man-made objects" Nashville, Tenn: American Assoc. for State and Local History.

Hey, M.H. (1955) "An index of mineral species and varieties arranged chemically" London: British Museum (Natural History) 2nd edn. 728pp.

M.D.A. (1981) "Guide to the Museum Documentation System" 2nd edn. Duxford, Cambridgeshire; England: Museum Documentation Association. 42pp.

Odin, G.S. (1982) "Numerical Dating in Stratigraphy" New York: John Wiley and Sons.

SHIC Working Party (1983) "Social History and Industrial Classification" Sheffield, England: Centre for English Cultural Tradition and Language. (from Museum Documentation Association)

Smither, R. (1985) "... transferring the documentation of the Imperial War Museum's film collection" M.D.A. Information vol 9, no 3. (Oct) p.67-74.

Vanns, M.A. (1984) "The general principles of SHIC" M.D.A. Information vol 8, no 2. p.32-35.

Chapter 9

Cumulative data

The reference framework for organising records in museums (REFORM) is designed with operational aspects of museum work in mind and in this respect it stands apart from many other schemes which offer only static record systems. In REFORM it is recognised that curatorial activity results in amendments being generated which make it necessary to insert supplementary data, eg reporting conservation measures, recent exhibitions, research and examinations of objects by visiting scholars, and newly discovered references in critical or technical literature, etc. The fundamental need arising from these activities is for a structure that allows additional data to be inserted into the existing records about individual objects. This is the purpose of the Third-Tier Sections. These are not the only ones to accommodate changes: there is another group of Sections comprising the Fourth Tier for dynamic data of a more ephemeral kind.

It is not always appreciated that there is a strong probability of changes being made to records after their initial creation because they include more than simply static descriptions. However, any exercise in re-cataloguing which includes inspection of old records provides ample evidence of the abundance of annotations post-dating the original documentation. Under traditional card filing methods it was not foreseen that revised opinion might require changes to the name by which an

141

object is known, or that more than one opinion of its proper designation can exist (in which case the rival attributions must be individually recorded).

Of course, in conventional filing systems changes and additions to information are not easily accommodated except by laborious alteration of typed data and by creating supplementary cards or storing additional documents in envelope files. However, the advent of computing systems suited to the office and work-place removes constraints that were inevitable when working with manual systems. The important thing is to perceive what is actually done by analysing the mental and manual operations from first creation of a new record to the maintenance of up-to-date information on files holding many thousands of records. The Third and Fourth Tiers of REFORM result from analysis of this kind.

Cumulative data are integral components of almost every object's record. The information held in Statements of the Third Tier is not concerned with the physical description of the objects but contributes particularly to knowledge about events involving them. In manual filing systems, this information may be stored in an envelope for each object into which correspondence, references and reports are filed. The five Statements within this Tier are designed to rationalise the miscellaneous data that accumulates in such files. One or more of them may resemble records to be found in the existing documentation of most museums, especially if they have a vigorous programme of changing exhibitions that is recorded or an active conservation unit with its own forms of object documentation: these account for two of the five Sections.

THE CONSERVATION SECTION   [Section   3.1.0]
This Section is intended to store not merely a single Statement but a series of Conservation Statements for every object handled in the studio or laboratory, each relating to a single incident in which the object is examined or treated. It may be conceived either as a constituent Section within the comprehensive record for each object or as a distinct file in which there are possibly several Statements relating to an object (each of them at different dates). Every Statement will contain some of the following Elements:

142

3.1.1   An essential Element of every Statement is the date at which the examination or treatment of the object was completed by a conservator. If this record is used to monitor the progress of treatment as it occurs, other time-related actions should be reported in addition, eg 3.1.8 ---date of request (submitting object for treatment); 3.1.9 --- date when treatment began; and ultimately, date of the object's return to curator (= relocation: 4.3.3).

3.1.2   Secondly the name of the conservator responsible for the work in hand needs to be stated (or if an external agency is used, the name of the laboratory or studio where the object was treated).

3.1.3   From the conservator's viewpoint it is desirable to record the name of the curator submitting the object for inspection and /or restoration.

Three Elements are reserved for use of controlled vocabulary to indicate respectively, the method of examination, method of treatment and the chemical reagents employed by the conservator; all of these requiring careful choice of terms involving technical processes.

3.1.4   Method of examination includes many instrumental techniques which are non-destructive and some which involve tests on small samples. For example, the method of examination may be described as 'visual' or, if instrumental inspection is used, it can be recorded by such terms as 'microscopy', 'endoscopy' (with technical details added), 'UV-fluorescence', 'X-ray', or even simply by 'weighing' or 'measurement' if these form part of an assessment of the object's condition. While verbose statements must be avoided here, it is useful to devise a syntax in which the keyword is followed by a concise note of technical detail, eg:

microscopy; plano objective x40/0.65.

3.1.5   Similarly, the method of treatment is best expressed by selecting the relevant term from a restricted vocabulary. For example, terms such as 'immersion', 'painting', 'injection', 'cleaning', 'fumigation' and other process descriptors can be applied. As before, it is possible by establishing suitable syntax conventions to include some additional detail with these keywords, eg "immersion, in vacuum chamber at 0.2 atmospheres".

In relation to museum exhibits that have been rebuilt by replacing parts or materials (as distinct from stabilising the original fabric), the appropriate keyword is 'restored'. It can be used as the leading term in an explanatory report of actions taken, eg (for a bicycle) "restored; spokes from rear wheel removed and replaced with heavier gauge".

3.1.6   The record of chemical reagents used is intended both as a report to curators and as technical data for retrieval by conservators. To ensure its successful performance in both these respects, there must be total control of the chemical vocabulary to avoid the occurrence of technical synonyms, especially in the naming of organic reagents. There is considerable advantage, in this situation, in using a computer system which checks words automatically against an authority file as data are entered.

3.1.7   When treatment is applied to an object, it is usually necessary to specify what part of the item was treated. On subsequent occasions, when an object is returned to the laboratory for further treatment, the area affected must again be stated because the cause and site of defect may be quite separate from those of previous treatments.

3.1.8   To manage a conservation workshop of any kind it is helpful to record the date of each request made by a curator (named in 3.1.3) which usually accompanies an object submitted for inspection and /or treatment. The entry of these two Elements (curator's name and date of request), together with the object's accession number, comprises a minimal record of work awaiting attention.

3.1.9   It is required practice in many studios and laboratories to record the date at which the conservation work commences. This Element is included for that purpose: it facilitates administrative review of work in progress. Another benefit is that retrospective reports can be analysed to compare the number of starts with requests received during the same period.

The practical nature of conservation work might suggest that data on this topic might be better located with other aspects of collection management.   While recognising its practical aspect, placement of the Conservation Section in the Third Tier of the reference framework is logically based on its requirements for information-handling.   Storage of conservation data as integral Statements within object records (or as separate records in independent files), differs essentially from records concerning loans, values and locations. Data on conservation treatments is cumulative and all of it remains relevant for reference in relation to future treatments of the same or other objects. It can be compared, therefore, with the documentation of exhibitions and with new reports on attribution, publications and reproductions of objects, in which data remains relevant long after the event.

THE ATTRIBUTION STATEMENT   [Section   3.2.0]

The precise meaning of 'Attribution' depends largely on the kind of collections we are dealing with. When comparing attributions in fine art and natural history, for example, the implications are superficially distinct but on logical analysis the function of attribution is the same in both disciplines. It is concerned with verifying the names with which objects are identified, also with attesting the authorship of man-made works and confirming date or place of origin by adducing evidence. In each of these various ways, attribution is the record of an opinion by a named person who is recognised as being competent to assess the circumstances relating to the object under review.

The Statement of Attribution (of which more than one may be filed for each object) consists of the following Elements:

3.2.1   Name of author of the opinion, ie expert or 'authority'. This is subject to the usual conventions governing personal names in order to assist retrieval.

3.2.2   The place with which the expert is affiliated, official address and /or position comprise the content of this Element. Circumstances require some flexibility here as it may accommodate just a city name or a full address, or even the official designation of the referee, eg "Director of the Hals Museum, Haarlem".

3.2.3   The date of his /her assessment of the object is entered.

3.2.4   The substance of the expert opinion expresses his /her assessment of whatever attribute is under consideration. As it applies to works of art and craftsmanship, this opinion is likely to confirm or refute the authenticity of the object. The expert may conclude that the work in question is a fake. This Element can be organised according to the convention in which the keyword is placed first, where it stands as a signal to the ensuing comment. With reference to The Water Mill by Hobbema, there is a more recent attribution than those quoted (Example 10) and this later Statement illustrates the method of structuring:

3.2.1 (author of opinion) Rickett, R C

3.2.2 (his affiliation)   Keeper of Fine Art, City Art Gallery

3.2.3 (date of opinion)   1981 Dec 9th

3.2.4 (text of opinion)   [keyword] fake; our picture is undoubtedly a copy, but an old one .... it having fallen from grace since its acquisition.

3.2.5 (documentation)   [keyword] letter   to   J.Shalding, Graves Art Gallery, Sheffield

3.2.5   As illustrated in the preceding paragraph, this Element is needed to record the medium or method in which the opinion was expressed. A determinate list of keywords may well be appropriate, including among others, 'letter', 'report', 'tape', 'oral' (spoken) etc. but if published give the full reference as a Citation (Section 3.4.0).

A narrative Statement of Attribution is easily segmented into its constituent Elements, as shown in the following: "John Baynes of the Royal Ontario Museum identified this piece as 2nd century North African red slip ware, and thought it unlikely to have been found in London".

3.2.1 = Baynes, John

3.2.2 = Royal Ontario Museum

3.2.3 = no date recorded for the opinion

3.2.4 = [keyword] identified; (opinion as follows) 2nd century North African red slip ware, unlikely found in London.

To demonstrate another use of the Attribution Statement, with reference to a boy's coat of presumed eighteenth century date, the reported opinion may relate to the precise period of manufacture, eg

"Dr. Cunnington, 1st April 1956, says date would be 1770-1780, as indicated by the back vents of the coat, where the material overlaps the vent; known technically as 'tack-over'. Also the side seams are placed far back, ... a method of construction unknown before 1770."

146

This whole Statement, except for the name "Dr. Cunnington" and date of his report, is included in Element 3.2.4, either in full or in condensed form. In this example, the decade to which the coat is referred would be used as the basis of classifying the garment by age (Element 2.2.2) in the Statement of Classification. By contrast, it is recommended that this date-range (1770-1780) should not appear in the Statement of Origin (under date of manufacture), where definite knowledge rather than surmise is required. It is quite possible for an article to be classified by age without a specific date being known for its origin. Thus, if properly used, each of the Sections has a part to play in the information structure and the whole system gains precision.

In collections of botanical, zoological and fossil material, the Attribution Statement makes provision for the re-naming of individual specimens when they are found to be mis-identified or when their names are re-determined in relation to a revision of taxonomic nomenclature. Thus the compilation of such Statements forms a record of opinion on identity and nomenclature throughout the specimen's history.

When a biological or geological object is re-identified, there is a choice to be made concerning the role the new designation will be given within the existing system of classification. The Linnean name recorded in Element 3.2.4 represents an authoritative view of the specimen's new classified position. The special merit of recording it as an Attribution Statement is that it is linked with the name of the person responsible for its determination. One option is to copy the new classified name into the Classification Section (Element 2.2.9) in substitution for the previously accepted name. However, an update of the classified name (if effected for individual records but not necessarily for all examples of the same species) disrupts the prevailing system of nomenclature by which the collection is named and arranged. A recommended alternative is not to introduce synonyms into the Classification (where all members of a species should appear under the same name) but to retain the most recent name in the Attribution Section where, with earlier opinions, it remains available for immediate retrieval.

THE EXHIBITION STATEMENT   [Section   3.3.0]

This Section holds a continuing record of all exhibitions in which each object has been shown, both within and outside the museum that owns it.   Such information is usually maintained by inserting supplementary notes on the record card giving details of each occasion when the work was exhibited.   In practice this is often inconvenient unless sufficient space has been reserved on the card for successive notes to be entered but with computerised methods expansion of existing data can be more easily managed.

3.3.1   The first Element must be the date of the exhibition; its precise form being a matter for local decision.   At a minimum it may be stated as year only or it can be expanded to include the complete dates of the exhibition's opening and ending.

3.3.2   There is usually a title for the exhibition, which is sometimes so widely promoted (eg internationally) that it serves as a major point of reference for the object itself.   This title constitutes the second Element.   The name of the host institute and the location of the exhibition are the remaining Elements needed to complete the Exhibition Statement.

3.3.3   The name of the exhibiting institute is normally recorded using the syntax of its official title.   However, even in this seemingly simple situation there are hidden complexities which can be resolved only by means of syntax conventions. Example: how is it best to record "University of California Museum of Cultural History, Los Angeles"? Some compression of a long title may be desirable and also selective exclusion of redundant names.   Perhaps in this example we may write, "Museum of Cultural History, UCLA".   Its geographical location (Los Angeles) belongs in the following Element.

3.3.4   The location of the exhibiting institute should be stated in accordance with an appropriate in-house convention naming either city or state first.

THE CITATION STATEMENT   [Section 3.4.0]

This Section enables citations to be included into an object's record of references to published and unpublished papers, articles, reviews, etc

148

in which that object is actually mentioned. Thus it links other Sections of the record with literature or extramural documentation of any kind. For example, it would be proper to include reference to an account of the origin of the 'Castle' design (Example 25b) and equally suitable to accommodate a citation referring to the location of various casts of the sculpture by Giacomo Zoffoli (Example 23). The standard Elements of each citation are those normally found in bibliographic references.

3.4.1   name(s) of author(s)

3.4.2   title of book, article or paper

3.4.3   name of periodical or (if a book) of publishing house

3.4.4   date of publication or (if unpublished) origination

3.4.5   place of publication or production

3.4.6   The sixth Element has an essential role in relating the cited work to the object which is the subject of the record. In fulfilling this role it may serve as a cross-reference to another Section. A short lexicon of terms is needed to describe the function each reference performs and how it relates to the object itself.

Thus, the term 'illustrated' should not imply merely that the cited paper contains illustrations but rather that it specifically illustrates the object. Alternative functions of citation include those where the object is 'described', 'mentioned' (ie referred to without full description) and others relating to various Sections, eg 'attribution reviewed','derivation reviewed', 'ownership reviewed', etc. It is not recommended to use this Section when citing works in which the particular object is not referenced, although publications giving details of similar examples may contribute to understanding of the item known to us.

THE FACSIMILE STATEMENT   [Section 3.5.0]

The function of this Section is to record the existence of faithful copies or derivatives of an object which are of such a standard that they constitute works of artistic or scientific merit in their own right. The most obvious examples are casts of a sculpture and replicate casts of fossilised skeletal specimens taken from the original bones. Replicas of both kinds are usually housed and exhibited at other institutions as museological objects. In effect this provides a concise directory of other venues where the same work can be seen and so there are as many Statements in this Section as there are known casts. For example, three casts of the Zoffoli bronze of Marcus Aurelius (Example 23) would be recorded in three Facsimile Statements, which provide the following information:

(a) 3.5.1 maker (?)   3.5.2 Kassel; Schloss Wilhelms-Hohe

(b) 3.5.1 Giao.Zoffoi F; signed   3.5.2 Dresden; Grune Gewolbe
     3.5.3 (date)   1764

(c) 3.5.1 G. Zoffoli F; signed   3.5.2 Devon; Saltram Park

The component Elements in each Facsimile Statement are defined as:

    3.5.1   who was the maker of the cast or print?
    3.5.2   where is the cast /replica /print located?
    3.5.3   when was it made /published?
    3.5.4   what method or process was used in its production?
    3.5.5   what title does it bear (if different from the original)?

In the case of records describing paintings and drawings which have been reproduced as prints, this Section serves to point to the existence of prints derived from the original work in our collection. References made to such prints could be restricted to those included in our museum's collection or, by policy, could include all derived prints known. "The Distressed Poet" painted by Hogarth (Example 9) was the subject of engravings by the same artist and the existence of these may be included in the record of the principal work (as its derivatives) in a series of Facsimile Statements, eg

    3.5.1   Hogarth, William
    3.5.2   ----
    3.5.3   1736 Mar 3rd
    3.5.4   line engraving
    3.5.5   The Distressed Poet

In many cases the maker of the engraving is not the artist of the prime work and therefore Element 3.5.1 may record various names with some indication of their respective roles,

    eg "Vertue G, sculpt and Greene W, delin".

150

The abbreviations are from the Latin and indicate the plate-maker and the draughtsman respectively. Reproduction of pictures or engravings in newspapers and magazines does not qualify for inclusion in this Section (which records only items that are themselves works of repute). Therefore, with reference to Example 9, reproduction of the Hogarth painting in The Times newspaper, 2nd August 1934, would not be treated as a facsimile but instead should be entered as a Citation Statement [Section 3.4.0] referring to an 'illustrated' publication.

Chapter 10

Managerial data

When record systems for museums are discussed it is usually on an assumption that the purpose of documentation is to catalogue collections. Another function on which attention is less often focussed is collection management: for this purpose we need to keep information of a dynamic kind and to update details that change in the course of normal museum routines. Movement of objects, from storage to exhibition, from cabinet to conservation laboratory, frequently go unrecorded and it is left to a curator's memory to recall where a particular item can be found. The capability of computers to serve as a substitute for the mental note-pad makes them an obvious solution for handling this type of data.

Valuation of objects in relation to insurance cover, if for no other reason, is liable to need reassessment and revision at periodic intervals yet it is a tedious task for curators that is often neglected. Loans of objects are not likely to be overlooked in well-organised record systems, as they are usually written in a ledger or card file separate from the catalogue, but confusion can arise if staff are not informed by circulating copies of new loan records or if data entry is delayed. Computing facilities open up the prospect of linking managerial requirements with the catalogue to form a comprehensive information system.

Fourth-Tier Sections in the reference framework REFORM contain Statements in which the information can change from time to time.

Detail changes affect only some Elements of these Statements and the frequency of changes depends on the incidence of curators' activities. In activities such as reappraisal of objects, transfer and movement of objects, revaluations and loans there is likely to be continual access to records on these aspects and frequent alteration of data to maintain current and valid information. In a curatorial context these activities are equivalent to 'transactions' in a commercial environment and possess the same characteristics in terms of data management.

An enquiry like "How many bronze palstaves are in drawers A-E in the Basement Store?" is exactly comparable with an airline booking enquiry, "How many first-class seats are available on Flight ELSA 109?" In both cases the answer is a number that is variable over time and the only information of relevance to the enquirer is the up-to-date value. In the airline office, yesterday's data are irrelevant today because those data are already obsolete. The time-scale in museums is different but data that answered the question six weeks ago are now probably obsolete (if items have been moved in or out of store in that interval).

Using the same analogy, we notice the essential similarity between other paired questions that can be asked in these two contrasting situations. For example, "What is the price of a first-class air fare from London to Amsterdam?" can be compared with "What is the current insured value of the painting ...?" In both cases only information that is current is of interest to the enquirer: the economy air-fare offered last month is irrelevant today! Similarly the old insurance value of a painting before it was revalued is also irrelevant to the continuing management of the collection.

In consequence of the dynamic character of data in Fourth-Tier Sections, provision must be made for obsolete data to be cancelled and replaced by current data. Although amendments needed to maintain up-to-date information in museums are not as frequent as with theatre or airline reservations, the facility must exist for convenient and prompt amendment of data in order to record the results of staff actions. In a manual card file of records (one card per object) the simplest means of amendment is to delete the existing statement, eg "Location: basement store 2A", and write beneath it the new statement, "Location: Egyptian

153

Gallery, 21/3/83". There are obvious limitations to the number of times such changes can be made unless adequate space is available on the card to allow successive amendments. REFORM emphasises the importance of ensuring that information about the current location is always available and that it is associated with related data. This benefit is optimised by transferring the structured data to computer.

The MDA record system makes no explicit reference to the design of files for routine procedures of collection management such as relocation, revaluation and administration of conservation work-in-progress and loans. It is acknowledged, however, (Roberts 1985) that "The scale of the maintenance problem (ie updating volatile information) has only been commonly appreciated in recent years when it has become apparent that a number of the first generation of automated systems are inefficient in dealing with dynamic records, having been designed on the false assumption that museum records are rarely revised ...."

In REFORM the data involved in managerial records are treated in exactly the same way as data contained in curators' catalogues: they are regarded as comprising Statements, each with its integral Elements. For managerial purposes, the dynamic records of Fourth-Tier Statements do not stand alone but must be capable of linkage with some Sections of lower Tiers. For example, we need cross-references between valuation and price paid (cf Acquisition), between loans and Exhibition (3.3.0) and between Identity (2.1.0) and various dynamic data. The modular form of the reference framework enables such relationships to be readily established, especially in computer-based systems, and yields immediate reports of related information for all managerial purposes.

In addition to the Sections already mentioned, there is a Status Section in which we record assessments of an object's condition, its potential as a museum exhibit and contingency for its eventual disposal.

THE STATUS SECTION   [Section   4.1.0]
The status of an object is subject to periodical revision. This can result in changes being made to the data recorded in this Statement by substitution of updated information, arising from re-assessment of the object in several respects.

154

4.1.1   The first Element describes the condition of the object by selecting the appropriate term from a list of standard descriptors, namely: 'mint', 'fine', 'good', 'fair', 'poor'. This keyword may be followed by an extended comment, if desired, to amplify the information; for example, "fine; glaze has superb lustre". The word 'fine' is the obligatory descriptor; the ensuing phrase is optional free-text.

In reference to the natural sciences, the status of a specimen has a special meaning which has no counterpart in disciplines that do not employ Linnean nomenclature. A specimen has unique importance if it is the one to which the scientific name was first given by the author of that name: it is then designated as the 'holotype'. Other variants indicate specimens which were in some degree recognised by the author of the name, eg 'lectotype', 'syntype', etc. Also signifying a high status for a specimen is the fact that it is 'figured' (=illustrated) or 'cited' in a scientific publication. These terms belong in Element 4.1.1 either in place of or immediately following the leading keyword used to specify condition.

4.1.2   The second Element is for remarks on the purpose for which the object is best suited among the various functions of collections. The following categories are offered as examples of the kind:

(a) 'Exhibit' category indicates that the qualities of the object as a whole suggest that it should be regarded as highly suitable for public exhibition when opportunity allows.

(b) 'Example' indicates that the object is less desirable for display or better suited for use in a tutorial situation where its features can be pointed out. Free-text comment can be added as trailing data, thus, "example; has display potential if re-enamelled".

(c) 'Special' category indicates that although the object does not have high visual interest for the wider purposes already mentioned, it possesses in a high degree features of interest for research study.

(d) 'Voucher' category indicates that the object is representative of its kind but its main interest may be circumstantial, ie relating to information on its use or origin, or simply as visible proof of its occurrence at a known place and time.

4.1.3   The third Element describes any physical defects that exist when objects are received or which occur subsequently, as in the event of accidental damage. It is preferable that one out of several permitted terms be stated first to indicate the nature of the defect, followed by some kind of expanded comment, eg (bicycle) "incomplete; saddle missing, some new spoking needed" or (clay tablet) "broken; lower left corner detached, also crack in lower right".   Standard descriptors include 'incomplete' when a constituent part is missing, 'broken' (when one or more pieces have become detached), 'damaged' (when disfiguring marks are visible), 'stained', 'faded', 'dented', 'abraded', etc.

4.1.4   The date of the report on Status is entered at the time when this description is written and a new date is substituted on any subsequent occasion when it is revised by re-assessment of the object, by change in its condition or by its disposal or loss.

It is not often that, after admission to the museum's collections, an object may need to be deleted from the list of current holdings. However, if a long-term loan is brought to an end by request of the owner of the loaned item, then that situation does occur.

4.1.5   When the object is disposed of by return to the lender (in the above case) or by other means in other circumstances, it is necessary to state the method of disposal or removal. This could be any one of: 'returned', 'transferred', 'destroyed', 'given', 'not found', 'stolen', or 'sold'. Additional comment can be made to follow any of these keywords, eg "not found when store cleaned".

4.1.6   To provide for transfer, return, gift or sale of an object to a person or institute, this Element provides space to record the name of the recipient.

4.1.7   If the object is sold, the price received for it is stated.

4.1.8   This Element allows note to be made of any conditions forming part of an agreement with the recipient of the disposed item. This Statement of disposal accords closely with the procedure suggested by Norgate (1984). Most importantly, when any object is "written off" the name of the curator responsible must be added; and this forms the final Element (4.1.9) of this Statement.

156

THE VALUATION STATEMENT   [Section   4.2.0]

When an object is initially valued and on subsequent occasions when its
value is re-assessed, a Valuation Statement is written. This comprises
just four Elements and, to create a valid Statement, it is obligatory that
all are completed on every occasion of assessment.

4.2.1   The object's assessed monetary value is recorded in
Element 4.2.1. This is supported by Element 4.2.2, giving the name of
the assessor (who may be a professional valuer or firm of valuers) or,
failing that, the name is given of the curator whose opinion of value is
represented.

4.2.3   In every case the date of valuation is recorded so that
revision may be effected on a sound basis of knowledge, relating the
value with the date when it was last assessed.

4.2.4   Lastly, where an individual insurance schedule is specific
to that object, the schedule number is reported. In default of a unique
number being allotted, the reference number of the general policy
covering all collections will be inserted.

It is clear from this account that several Valuation Statements may
be made over a period of years, all relating to the same object but each
distinguished by its date. Only the most recent of these will be kept
on file because a re-valuation renders obsolete the earlier Statement in
this Section of the record. When a new Valuation Statement is submitted
therefore, the previous data are deleted from the record and the new
data substituted. This is one reason why the authority for each and
every valuation shall be stated as an integral part of the record.

THE LOCATION STATEMENT   [Section   4.3.0]

When an object is registered or as soon as possible thereafter, when its
location has been decided, a Location Statement is written. This Section
is highly important because it will be read in conjunction with the
valuation data in the process of audit. It also serves as a practical aid
to the curator by enabling lists to be created of all objects housed in
the same location. The Elements are:

4.3.1   Element 4.3.1 records the place where the object is
normally kept, ie its permanent home as distinct from any temporary

157

placements that occur from time to time. It names the gallery location if the object is normally on exhibition and records the storage location if the object is usually kept as part of a reference or reserve collection. Exhibits located at branch museums are recorded by firstly entering the name of the building where they are housed, then naming the room in which they are shown /kept. Indeed, recommended data for every location include 'building', 'floor' and 'room' (abbreviated or coded if necessary).

4.3.2   The storage position within the store-room (or display position within the gallery) should be given precisely by reference to shelf, cabinet and drawer (or exhibition case number).

4.3.3.   The date at which the object was placed there is next recorded. This date is subject to amendment in relation to the following Element and to any subsequent movements between the two locations.

4.3.4   This Element provides for recording temporary changes of location, for example, when an object is moved from its normal site to be included in a temporary exhibition or removed from storage to conservation workrooms for inspection, restoration or remedial treatment. When relocation involves the transference of an object from one building to another, this Element includes firstly the name of the building to which it is transferred and secondly the name of the room within it.

4.3.5   If more precise detail is needed, eg exact location in temporary storage, this information can be assigned to Element 4.3.5 which holds data comparable to that for permanent locations detailed in 4.3.2 above.

Whenever an amendment is made necessary by re-location, either permanent or temporary, the date previously entered in this Statement is revised to correspond with the current position. When an object is returned to its normal location from internal exhibition, curator's office or conservation laboratory, the date of its return should be notified and the record of temporary location deleted. By this simple method the present location of an object will always be known.

To provide a high degree of control over object movements, as may be necessary in larger museums employing numerous personnel, it is desirable that the current location should be certified by a person with appropriate authority. In effect, what is needed is the equivalent of a signature to confirm that the object has been received by the department accepting it (on return from loan, on delivery to the studio for conservation, etc). At its simplest, this can be achieved by including

4.3.6   an additional Element (4.3.6) in which to record the name of the officer who verifies the object's position. However, to avoid misuse of this facility (a 'forged signature') in systems where security is paramount, confirmation can be entered in encrypted form if the record is entered on computer.

THE LOAN STATEMENT   [Section   4.4.0]

The situation relating to records of loans is directly comparable to a business transaction, eg in a vehicle leasing company, the only difference being that the museum is not raising revenue from outward loans. In terms of data management the absence of a financial element makes no difference at all: in other respects the data elements of the two transactions are the same. Dates of reservation, of shipment and recall are precisely comparable in the two situations. Both records include the name and address of the borrower/lessee and of insurance arrangements in force for the duration of the loan contract. In museums as in commerce, the relevant records are those referring to active loans, ie of objects currently in the custody of the borrower. When an item is returned and checked-in, the record remains of interest only as a statistic in the annual report of loans issued. There can be little purpose in retaining such records beyond the end of the financial year or period of report to the museum's trustees. When the same item is loaned again (more frequently, we hope, for the leasing company than for the museum) the new record displaces the previous one on the file.

The administration of loans is a normal part of curators' duties and it is usually accomplished by keeping a Loans Register in which all out-going objects are recorded or by completing some kind of form with copies sent to administrators and insurers. It is unlikely that this function alone would justify the introduction of computers because the frequency of loans made between museums does not bear comparison with leasing of vehicles or the lending of books by libraries. However,

159

in association with other dynamic aspects of collection management, loan arrangements can be better controlled by computer-aided methods.

A Loan Statement is created on each occasion that a loan request is fulfilled. The majority of these relate to outward loans, in which the duration and conditions are determined by the lending institution. Inward loans of a temporary kind are also recorded in this Section but those objects accepted as inward loans of long duration are better recorded as accessions to the institute's collections and must be the subject of Acquisition Statements (q.v.).

4.4.1   The first Element states what object(s) or part(s) of the object is to be loaned or borrowed, as applicable. For inward loans (short-term) this is the only place in which the Brief Description of the borrowed item or its name or title is registered, so it is an essential Element.

4.4.2   The name of the borrower (or lender's name in the case of inward loans) is entered in accordance with a general convention on personal names.

4.4.3   A separate Element for the destination of the item loaned (if outward) or address for correspondence.

4.4.4   It is useful to record the purpose of the loan, eg study or exhibition. This Element includes less obvious reasons for outward loan, eg for radiocarbon dating or special conservation work.

4.4.5   The distinction between inward and outward loans is made in Element 4.4.5, which also states the duration of the period of loan, eg 'OUT 6 months' (or 'OUT 6 mth'). For reasons already given it is unlikely to be measured in years (see Element 1.1.1).

Then follow three Elements for operative dates that are useful for listing and on computer systems can prompt when action is required:

4.4.6   date when the loaned object was dispatched (received if inward loan);

4.4.7   date when the loaned object becomes due for return;

4.4.8   date when the loan was actually returned/ received on its return.

These loan data make it possible in computerised systems to obtain reports in listed formats to suit a variety of practical purposes. These

160

can assist staff to discover the details of an outstanding loan, signalled by its 'due date', and also to check the whereabouts of any object that is at an extramural location (for whatever reason). Thus it can be used as an adjunct to the Location Section of the record which (in distinction) registers all intramural situations.

MANAGERIAL REPORTS

The partitioning of Statements into Elements confers flexibility, making it possible to retrieve only those data that are relevant to an enquiry. With reference to managerial data, Elements needed to provide current information on various aspects of collection management can be extracted from the reference framework and assembled in suitable format to create reports. For a majority of administrative purposes it is possible to devise standard report formats, each one being suitable for reviewing values and loans issued.

Those Elements that are subject to the operation of conventions in formal mode, eg dates, are usually brief and of known length. This is true of determinate Elements, in which data are reduced to a single word selected from a fixed vocabulary of approved terms. Elements of both types feature prominently in managerial reports and are well suited for tabulated arrangement, in which data are listed in columns under appropriate headings (each representing one Element).

To construct tabular reports of this kind it is only necessary to select the Elements to be included and to decide the best order of columns from left to right. Simple as this may seem, as space across the page is limited by paper width, it is advisable to establish a sound reason for admitting each Element chosen for inclusion, omitting those that are not essential for the purpose(s) that the report will serve. The purpose of a report must be clearly identified in terms of "what we want to know" before its composition is defined and its format set up. The designer of a report should consider carefully the following points.

(i) Which data will be the leading Element; ie in the first column? The Element selected for this role is the primary key, giving access to correlated data in adjoining columns. The primary key can be sorted into either alphabetical or numerical sequence (depending on the chosen data) to aid visual searching as in a telephone directory.

(ii) Which of the other data may also be required in sorted order? These Elements serve as secondary keys and may be sequenced either in combination with the prime key or as alternatives to the primary sequence when a variant of the normal report is needed.

Example A

Purpose of Report: to report all loans issued in the first half-year. The requisite records are those qualified by the keyword OUT, which indicates outward loans (Element 4.4.5) and by date of issue (Element 4.4.6) which must fall between 1st January and 30th June of this year.

The relevant data for inclusion in this report are:

a) identity of object. Unique identifier is Accession No. (2.1.1)
b) identity of borrower. (4.4.2)
c) period of loan. (4.4.5)
d) due date for return. (4.4.7) This is essential to monitor compliance and, in default, to prompt the borrower.
e) date received on return. (4.4.8) Confirms return of the object to its normal location (4.3.1).

Additional Elements for optional inclusion might be:

f) purpose of loan (4.4.4) May be useful if reporting to Committee.
g) defects noted on return. (4.1.3) May serve to prompt a claim on the insurer or placement on a waiting list for repair /restoration.

The primary key in this report is usually the name of the borrower: certainly we shall want to see all objects that were loaned to the same institute (or individual) listed consecutively and therefore the records must be sorted into sequence on this Element. Secondarily we want to list the identity of the objects loaned and for convenience these too should be sorted into ascending numerical order for each borrower. This is an example of combined sorting by two criteria. The resulting report appears in Table (A).

Example B

Purpose of Report: to select items from store for exhibition. The general category of material being sought is defined by suitable

162

TABLE (A)

Name of Borrower (4.4.2)	Object Number (2.1.1)	Period of Loan (4.4.5)	Date Due (4.4.7)	Returned (4.4.8)
Halton House Museum	1006	OUT 6mth	29 Oct 1986	------------
Halton House Museum	2562	OUT 6mth	29 Oct 1986	------------
Orion Gallery	6120	OUT 3mth	30 Jun 1986	10 Jul 1986
Orion Gallery	6693	OUT 3mth	30 Jun 1986	10 Jul 1986
Orion Gallery	6787	OUT 4mth	20 Oct 1986	------------
Raikes, O H K	3129	OUT 1mth	10 Jul 1986	9 Jul 1986
Smallhouse, P Ms.	4508	OUT 4mth	18 Sep 1986	13 Sep 1986
Trencham, W M Dr.	6372	OUT 4mth	8 Sep 1986	------------

TABLE (B)

Normal Location (4.3.1)	Shelf Position (4.3.2)	Temporary Location (4.3.4)	Object Number (2.1.1)	Object Class (2.2.9)
Basement Rm 5	K20	-----	11160	figurine
Basement Rm 5	L08	-----	12601	cylinder seal
Basement Rm 5	L12	-----	38080	figurine
Basement Rm 5	L13	-----	03330	figurine
Basement Rm 6	A04	-----	63505	vessel
Basement Rm 6	A06	Gallery 24	41804	trumpet
Gallery 10	-----	-----	54097	coffin
Strongroom	box 16	-----	00987	necklace

keywords in the Statement of Classification (Elements 2.2.7; 2.2.8; 2.2.9) and material of exhibition quality is signalled by the keyword 'exhibit' in Element 4.1.2. The relevant data for inclusion are:

a) identity of object. Unique identifier is Accession No. (2.1.1)

b) precise class of object (2.2.9) as an aid to recognition.

c) normal storage location. (4.3.1)

d) precise storage position. (4.3.2)

e) temporary location, (4.3.4) for items not found in normal location. Additional Elements which might be included optionally are:

f) condition of object (4.1.1)

g) display category (4.1.2) if 'exhibit' was not specified. The report will be best suited to the practical task of searching storerooms if records are sequenced in order of rooms (this being the prime key) and sorted by order of storage position within each room, taking shelves or cabinets in numerical sequence (secondary key). The resulting report appears in Table (B).

Under computer control, the same form of report can be simply adapted to create a directory to locations for an entire collection. This is achieved by re-sequencing the report by sorting the records into numerical order on object number (which thus becomes the prime key). The report now serves to index the location of any individual object. It is not even necessary to reformat the report by moving the column of data for Object Number to the left of the table: it is equally legible with the order of columns unchanged.

These illustrations preface a broader discussion of reports in the next chapter but, in demonstrating the good use to which dynamic data can be applied, they substantiate the value of the managerial Sections placed in the Fourth Tier of REFORM.

———————————

REFERENCES

Norgate, M. (1984) "Documentation in pastoral care museums -- disposal records" M.D.A. Information vol.8 no.1 p.23-26.

Roberts, D.A.(1985) "Planning the Documentation of Museum Collections" Cambridge, England: Museum Documentation Association.

Chapter 11

Meeting requirements

A manual system of documentation is not necessarily ineffective but, if it is fully competent, it is likely to involve many people in work that is labour-intensive and clerically routine. There are many possible factors that contribute to the realisation that processing records by present procedures (under manual systems) is actually inefficient and overdue for reform. It may be that problems have arisen due to a longstanding situation in which the documentation of objects in the museum and art collections has been gradually dispersed in consequence of organisational changes, eg through the evolution of new departments; or perhaps the production of records has become subject to delays caused by increased complexity in the organisation or by shortages of staff or funding. An appraisal of existing documentation may reveal some of the following features that raise questions about the efficiency of existing methods. A combination of several or all of these features indicates an assemblage of information sources which is inefficient, less than effective and both difficult and costly to maintain.

a)   A typed or written register of all items received into the museum's collections contains essential information that is of permanent value and importance. However, it is a static document usually in bound volumes which are never updated: it therefore excludes information that is liable to change.

b)   A register is sequenced necessarily in date order according with the order of registration of items received. This arrangement is not suitable for the majority of enquiries because information can be retrieved only by knowing either the unique number assigned to each object or the approximate date of its acquisition.

c)   In most cases, retrieval requirements are satisfied by referring to more comprehensive records held on catalogue cards filed in classified arrangement and additionally served by indexes.

d)   Card catalogues and indexes, however, may be dispersed in offices and workrooms for the convenience of curatorial control of access to them but with consequent difficulty for cross-referencing. Possibly no common standards are observed in compiling and maintaining them.

e)   Dispersed card indexes and documentary files hold current data on volatile aspects of record which cannot be conveniently amended on the main catalogue card or on fixed pages in bound volumes.

f)   Practical difficulties of maintaining a register, inventory, indexes and paper files may be shown by growth in arrears of processing new registrations or by failure to update these various records.

g)   In some institutions (not only the smaller museum) no personnel are employed exclusively on originating records, on typing records or updating these: the work is distributed (with a multitude of other duties) among all clerical and professional staff and possibly no one has an overall view or overall responsibility.

GENERAL OBJECTIVES AND BENEFITS

The principal task to be achieved is one of consolidation, involving the retrospective conversion of existing documentation into a form that is retrievable by computer, to serve the varied requirements of technical and professional staff responsible for the care of collections. The prospect of undertaking this task may prompt the museum's directorate to re-examine and clarify responsibilities for all phases of documentation. Rationalisation of records and record-keeping procedures inevitably calls for resources in personnel, time and finance. It must be planned and co-ordinated as a project with clear objectives and leadership. The

166

project can be structured in two stages which will be subject to distinct schedules for operational and resource reasons.

The first stage includes three objectives:-

a)   to produce an agreed Requirements Definition;

b)   to identify and evaluate alternative solutions;

c)   to recommend a preferred solution with reasons.

The second stage will include:

d)   obtaining approval of trustees, committee, etc;

e)   ordering, delivery and installation;

f)   induction training and implementation.

The most important step to be taken towards meeting the museum's requirements for collection-based information is to assess exactly what its requirements are! This seems too obvious to deserve mention but it is often overlooked or perhaps avoided in the hope that assumptions will be sufficient substitute for analysis, which regrettably they never are. No really effective progress can be made towards setting up a new information system or totally revising and remodelling an old information system until the requirements have been stated. The consequence is that a hard and penetrating examination must be made of the institute's objectives and its functions in relation to its clients and its governing authority. The examination can be advanced by answering a series of questions which are linked to one another as shown in Figs. 1 and 2.

The Requirements Definition will define in detail the functional characteristics of an information system which incorporates all essential aspects of existing manual systems. As a preliminary to that task, it is helpful to summarise in broad terms the achievements that must result from the successful completion of a computerisation project. They include the following desirable objectives:

1.   Combine existing documentary sources into a unified information system relating all aspects of collected objects.

2.   Provide access to information on collected objects by reference to any expression contained in existing documentary sources (or by such selected criteria as may be specified).

3.   Enable logical groupings of records to be made on demand by

167

Figure 1   A SINGLE-TARGET INFORMATION SYSTEM

	Curators OR	Conservators OR	Admin/Audit OR	Public/Clients
WHO IS IT TO SERVE?				
HOW WILL ACCESS be offered?	ON-line + local printer	ON-line + Hard Copy	OFF-line Hard Copy	ON-line Viewdata
HOW IS CONTROL effected?	Password + Locked Files	Password + Locked Files	Restricted Distribution	by Screen Menu + Program
WHAT DEMANDS ARE KNOWN?	Source Register Class Catalogue Complete record Loan Register	Location list Inventory Treatment history Exhibit history	Source Register Inventory Insurance Loan Register	Class Catalogue Manufacturer Exhibit Location
WHICH DATA ARE NEEDED?	Identity Acquisition Ownership Description Classification Origin Discovery Maker's Mark Location Exhibition Status Attribution Association Derivation Citation Facsimile	Identity Exhibition Status Conservation Location	Identity Acquisition Loans Valuation Location	Identity Classification Origin Imagery Location (part) Discovery

Figure 2

A MULTI-TARGET INFORMATION SYSTEM

WHO IS IT TO SERVE?	Curators + Technical	Curators, Technical + Admin/Audit	Museum Public, Curators + Admin/Audit
HOW WILL ACCESS be offered?	OFF-line Hard Copy	ON-line + Hard Copy	ON-line + local Printers
HOW IS CONTROL effected?	Restricted Distribution	Password + Locked Files	by Password on View/Amend/Print + Locked Files
WHAT DEMANDS ARE KNOWN?	Catalogue record Source Register Loan Register Storage lists	Source Register Loan Register Insurance lists Conservation lists Inventory record	1. Classified record 2. Complete record 3. Insurance lists 4. Conservation lists 5. General Enquiry
WHICH DEMANDS will be answered?	ALL	ALL	1,3,4,5
WHICH DATA ARE NEEDED?	Acquisition Ownership Identity Description Origin Discovery Location Loans	Acquisition Ownership Identity Location Conservation Valuation Status Loans	Acquisition Valuation Ownership Conservation Identity Status Description Location Origin Loans Discovery Attribution Imagery Citation Classification Facsimile

169

reference to classificatory terms, either extracted from or attached to existing text.

4. Improve and standardise methods of recording and revising data relevant to the control and management of collected objects.

5. Respond on demand to information requests, both general and specific, to meet the requirements of the target groups of users, eg:
   a) Auditors
   b) Conservators and technical staff
   c) Keepers and curatorial staff
   d) Museum visitors and the general public

General benefits to be gained from a computerised record system are improved control of valuable collections, improved efficiency in their management and improved service to the clientele through promotion and dissemination of cultural information. Particular benefits include:-

(i) Confidential data can be separated from publicly available data, recognising 'reserved' and 'open-access' categories respectively. This may lead to the establishment of a general policy, if one does not already exist, controlling disclosure of information. The more comprehensive computer systems provide mechanisms for controlling access to confidential information, either by means of passwords or by holding a file for every permitted user (who must identify him/ herself when logging-on). In that file, data access privileges are authorised to individuals or to groups of users who share the same identity: data categories which are not authorised in a user's file remain inaccessible.

(ii) Current data can be made available to authorised personnel without the obstacles and inconvenience of consulting card files dispersed among individual offices. One of the most limiting aspects of card catalogues and paper files is that the intending user so often must depend on the goodwill of a colleague to gain access to files about which that person has proprietory instincts.

(iii) Object movements can be better controlled because the system is much more responsive to amendment, whether for permanent trans- fer of whole collections or temporary moves of individual items. Of course, it is possible to have effective control under manual

170

systems, eg by use of a tally, but this is rather exceptional and, in many cases, movement records are less effective than they could be because they are tedious to maintain.

(iv) Ease of data revision must be one of the principal benefits derived from use of computers and its advantages will be known in every office where the typewriter has been replaced by electronic word-processor.

(v) Response to enquiries and service requests from other institutions (eg for loans) is improved both in speed and in the quality of reply. Recall of data can be accurate and comprehensive at the same time, which is rare in manual systems.

WHO IS THE INFORMATION USER?

The leading question looks directly to the ultimate user of information by asking who is the information intended to serve? To point the way to answering this, we can take a preliminary step by deciding whether the system is aimed at a particular user group or at several distinct groups, each having different interests. When these groups have been recognised, they should be regarded as the targets at which information is directed and for whom the system is designed to process and prepare that information.

If it is thought that the system has only a single target group, it should be a simple matter to identify the group by name. It is likely to be found among options such as clients (which includes academic researchers, students and a wider public), curators, conservators, technicians, administrators and governing bodies. Alternatively, if two or more of these groups are potential users of the system then we have to provide a multi-target system, which inevitably will be more complex. Those groups that will be users must now be named because the following questions to be answered relate explicitly to them and to no others.

Having decided who the users are, the next thing to consider is how will access to information be offered to the user? The user may have either open access or privileged access to printed data or to other forms of 'hard copy' such as microfiche. Otherwise, the user may have access to a computer terminal or visual display presenting information 'on-line', perhaps as 'viewdata' or in interactive mode responding to questions and instructions via a keyboard.

A further question that is closely linked to the last one is how will access be controlled? If a recognised group is named as the target user, it may be necessary to exclude non-members of that group from gaining access to the data. At this strategic stage in the development of a definition of requirements we are simply determining the general type of provision needed to make the information available. It may be that we plan to install a computer terminal in every curator's office but we should also consider how information will be delivered to technicians and to members of the public. For example, will periodical issues of a printed directory or report serve their requirements, whether by open access or with circulation limited to authorised personnel? Distinction must be made between confidential and publicly available data and museum obligations under the Data Protection Act (1984) be taken into account.

COMPREHENSIVE OR SELECTIVE INFORMATION?

When answers to the preceding questions have been resolved, thought can be given to what information the system should incorporate. As a preliminary step, what we need to decide is whether it will contain data on all aspects of museum objects or be restricted to selected aspects for limited purposes or for a single user group? If the latter choice is made, there is a further question that cannot be ignored for reasons of practical importance. Assuming that the museum already compiles data of an extensive kind about objects in its collections, it must be considered how the residual parts of this information will be processed and recorded if only selected aspects are to be entered onto computer. Consider for a moment whether the same or other clerical staff may have to process the residual data according to old established routines. The choice you make (comprehensive or selective) could increase the workload for the available staff and inevitably it has implications for organisation and allocation of duties among personnel. It could be self-defeating to introduce a scheme of intentionally limited extent, using computer facilities, while excluding some aspects of data which

172

the museum cannot totally neglect. In that situation, it will remain necessary to continue to process those residual data and the clerical work involved will absorb valuable paid time. A bad decision could result in maintaining two information systems, one efficient and computerised and the other inefficient and under-provided with resources. The conclusion is that a decision on what information is to be included should be taken in full knowledge of the staff resources available to be devoted to record maintenance as a continuing function. In any case, clerical staff will have to become accustomed to new methods and duties.

Decisions reached on the preceding questions establish a strategy for the information services to be provided, both for the museum's clients and for its staff. Within limits drawn by financial and human resources, informed by an awareness of future aspirations, it is now appropriate to look in detail at the information itself and to decide what should be included in the records.

Investigation of information requirements in relation to declared objectives is the business of information consultants and, in absolute terms, there are rather few of them who have any acquaintance with the museum scene. Even if the museum intends to engage consultants, it is necessary for curators to provide them with a factual appraisal of recognised demands which the projected system must answer. The first step to be taken is to identify in principle the nature of the demands made on existing resources by the public clientele and by the functions of collection management. The various channels of demand issuing from different sources must be separately described, not forgetting those demands that cannot be successfully answered under the prevailing methods of catalogue organisation.

It has already been decided what target group the system will support. We have now identified more precisely the demands issuing from that group. Having recognised the nature of the information being sought, it is a matter of logical analysis to determine which of the Statements of REFORM and, ultimately, which individual Elements of information (each of them numbered within REFORM) should be included in constructing the system. The most appropriate Elements from which this choice may be made for the major types of museum collections are

173

set out in tabular form in Appendix II as a guide to data definition.

On a broader front it may be helpful to notice that certain target groups of information users are generally concerned with data residing in one particular Tier of the REFORM model. For example, managers of collections require the Dynamic data described in Chapter 10, while in contrast, the museum visitor needs Descriptive data drawn from Second-Tier Statements described in Chapter 8. Researchers have greater need for the Historical and Cumulative data described in Chapters 7 and 9 respectively.

DELIVERING THE RESPONSE

In addition to determining the substantial content of the records, while planning an information system we must consider what methods are best suited for delivering the response to specific enquiries and for general dissemination of routine reports. Certain information users such as governing boards and committees have generalised needs for information in the form of routine reports at regular intervals, monthly, quarterly or annually. For example, they may require listings of all accessions of objects received since the previous report. In some respects this is a different requirement from that of auditors or curators. The frequency of demand is relevant to the choice of the reporting method. Where the demand is periodic, requiring a survey of actions taken, events elapsed or records entered since last report, it is obviously convenient to issue the relevant information in printed form, known as 'hard copy' as distinct from transient display on the computer screen. In such cases the routine nature of the demand means that a standard form of report is the best method of response.

Where the response must inform an entire group of persons and not just an individual, obviously a printed report is the only possible solution. There is another situation in which a printed report is needed but it is far from standard in format and data content. This occurs when we receive requests of a non-routine kind from a correspondent (ie mailed enquiry), frequently quite specific on the data required.

Contrasting with the above conditions, there are circumstances in which a more immediate (ie urgent) response is demanded and repeated demands are frequent but irregular. This situation can be handled in two ways. If the subject and data required are predictable, and if the relevant records remain unchanged by amendment, a printed copy can be made available for consultation at any time. For example, if we know from prior experience what the common topics of enquiry from members of the visiting public are, we can produce a ready-reference directory either in printed form or as a microfiche edition. On the other hand, internal demands of an ad hoc nature relating to the work of curators, conservators and technicians can only be effectively answered by on-line search and retrieval because the retrieval process proceeds interactively, refining the search by successive approximation. In this mode the group of objects can be optimally defined to yield a precise answer to what may be a very subtle enquiry.

Another aspect of the question (how to deliver the information) depends on whether the records answering the query relate to objects known to exist in the collection (and identifiable by reference number or by the name of donor or benefactor). To illustrate the point, let us suppose that a museum assistant moves objects in a store-room and he re-locates onto a new shelf a glass vase which he identifies by the number marked on its base (or on its label). His requirement is to call up the specific record relating to that object and to no other: only one unique record can fill this requirement. Similarly if a visitor requests to see the jewelled locket presented by her grandmother, we must be able to retrieve the appropriate record solely by reference to the name of that person.

By contrast, in other cases the enquirer (who may be a curator or a casual visitor) does not have prior knowledge that items possessing the qualities required actually exist in the museum's collection. The query therefore takes the form of an open question. It can be stated either as "Are there any silver coins from Roumania in the collection?" or else as "How many silver three-penny coins are there and what are their dates?" The answer to questions such as these may be a number of records anywhere between none and several hundreds. The best method of delivering such quantitatively variable data depends upon the purpose for which it is needed. Curators certainly need the option to

175

inspect retrieved records on-line and may also need printed copy for further reference. A member of the visiting public, researcher or student might be well satisfied with use of the same facility to browse through the relevant records on-line so that he /she may discover the few of greatest interest among the many retrieved by the search. In that case, certain reserved categories of data which are accessable to curators would not be retrieved by a visitor. Alternatively, visitors' enquiries can be met on a more restricted scale by providing bound copies of computer output reports indexed by the criteria most often in demand.

Lastly, in regard to delivery of the response, a fundamental choice has to be made between retrieving entire records (or entire paragraphs or Statements) and the quite different retrieval of selected data about objects. The latter option is achieved by isolating Elements within records and extracting those desired for a particular report (whether printed or displayed). The choice may well depend on decisions already taken about the extent and composition of data to be included in the records. For example, if the Statements to be included are mainly Historical or Descriptive (cf Chapters 7 and 8) a 'document storage' technique may be suitable. This is also appropriate if there is no requirement for sorting records into alphabetic or numeric series (other than the original order of input) and where emphasis is placed on the display of all information held about an object. However, if information is to be delivered in more digested form, with the salient facts distilled from the bulk of data recorded about each object, then the technique of storing and manipulating Elements of data must be adopted. This is emphatically the case if there is need for listing records in sorted arrangement according to various attributes of the objects.

REFERENCES

Baker, Christine (1984) "Human Aspects of Online Information Retrieval"
          p.122-133 in New Information Technology, edited by
          Alan Burns.

Burns, Alan [editor] (1984) "New Information Technology"
          Chichester, England: Ellis Horwood.   245pp.
          New York: Halsted Press, a division of J. Wiley & Sons.

Corbin, John (1981)   "Developing Computer-based Library Systems"
          Phoenix, Arizona: Oryx Press 214pp.

Hunter, E.J. (1985)   "Computerised Cataloguing"
          London: Clive Bingley   215pp.

Mitev, N.N.; G.M.Venner and S.Walker (1985)
          "Designing an Online Public Access Catalogue"
          Boston Spa, England: The British Library
          Library and Information Research Report 39.

Norman, Mike (1984)   "Organisational Requirements"   p.61-82   in
          New Information Technology, edited by Alan Burns.

Orna, E. and C.Pettitt (1980)   "Information Handling in Museums"
          London: Clive Bingley. New York: K.G.Saur.   190pp.

Roberts,D.A. (1985) "Planning the Documentation of Museum Collections"
          Cambridge, England: Museum Documentation Assoc. 568pp.

Townley, Helen M. (1978) "Systems Analysis for Information Retrieval"
          London: Andre Deutsch, in association with the Institute
          of Information Scientists. 120pp.

Chapter 12

Computer strategy

Museums have often found the transition to a computerised information system to be a traumatic experience and this is evident even in the restrained language of professional communication. "With hindsight, it is probably true to say that neither the Museum nor the M.D.A. fully appreciated the magnitude of the undertaking ..... Although progress has been made, it has not been as rapid as the Museum or the M.D.A. might have hoped ..... there have, indeed, been times when the most positive aspect of our advance does seem to have been that ..... we were not going backwards" (R Smither, 1985). This statement actually refers to the work of transferring records created under one computer system to a different system offered as a bureau service. The Imperial War Museum in London, whose experience was thus described, has been a pioneer institution among British museums (beginning in the late '60s) and its hard-won battle honours hold lessons for all who are involved in planning to introduce computers for documentation (cf. Smither, 1986). The starting point for computerisation is peculiar to each museum but unforeseen difficulties can be minimised by taking the trouble to examine intentions rigorously and, with the benefit of others' experience in their engagement with the task, to study the technical means now available to implement them.

DATABASE SYSTEMS ON COMPUTER

There are already several publications aimed at museum personnel which review the essential features of computers as devices for handling information about collected objects. In this regard it is sufficient to mention the important contributions of Sarasan and Neuner (1983), Roberts (1985) and the more general introduction given by Wilson (1986). However, the writer feels that there remains a proportion of curators for whom explanation must be made more immediate and practical, with illustrative reference to the kind of files they know and comprehend.

The central purpose of using computers in museums is to make accessible the information already held in massive archives of documentary material. The same can be said for the proceedings of the British Parliament, published daily in a journal known as 'Hansard', which is now available for consultation on computer as a 'database' (in one sense of that word). The whole text of debates in the House of Commons is stored on computer media in digital form and the subject-matter can be accessed by any significant word contained in the reported debates. Free-text search is ideally suited to this situation. To consult the database when seeking information on a topic, we use the computer's query facility to enter the words which indicate the matter of interest, in the expectation that it will retrieve some relevant material. Depending on the choice of keywords used to initiate the search, we often find that there is an excessively large volume of material to read through (some of it possibly superfluous). On the other hand, if there are few retrieved documents we may have doubts that all the material has been found: this can be a consequence of choosing search terms that do not coincide exactly with the expression used in the documents themselves. However, in most cases the retrieved material will satisfy the request, certainly when opportunity exists to refine the search words chosen by specifying a more selective term and running a second search through the records already retrieved at the first attempt.

This is somewhat different from the case when the enquirer knows the name of a member of Parliament whose speech relates to the topic. In this situation the enquirer can be fairly sure that by specifying

179

the Member's name for the computer search the appropriate report will be retrieved. The circumstances in museums often resemble the latter situation (when it is known that objects given by a named benefactor are present in the collections). In such cases, we can retrieve information by reference to a particular word which we know is included in all records to which it applies. This is a more positive strategy than casting hopefully for a word which may or may not be present or which may be represented in a sense by synonyms, if only we knew which ones.

The contrast between these approaches is illustrated by an analogy. Retrieving data by free-text search is like casting a net repeatedly into a broad and productive lake in the expectation of catching enough fish to load the cart for market: each cast captures more fish to be added to the total catch. Retrieving desired data from museum archives is more like draining a fishpond through a net with a mesh designed to catch all fish above a certain size. We know that such fish are in the pond but none must escape and the task is to isolate them from the remainder. There is a further possibility on computer which is scarcely feasible in a real-life fishpond: it is as if we had stocked the pond with individually weighed and marked fish. This allows us to catch them one by one and we can choose the fish for today's menu by weight or even by lucky number (a lottery on individual identity tags)!

Each of these situations is different and it is not surprising that computer systems designed to handle information ('information management systems') are modelled primarily upon one or another of these analogues. A system that is optimised for one strategy of "fishing" cannot be equally appropriate for alternative methods of data retrieval.

In the terminology of computer software the name 'database' applies to a narrowly defined concept. It is not wise to assume that it will provide just the requirements you had in mind. For the unsuspecting, a distinction must be made between database management systems and information storage and retrieval systems. This restricted vision of database is analogous to the third method of fishing the pond: if the individual weight or tag number of a fish is not known, then it cannot be caught (ie Retrieval is only possible by prescribed routes.). Most

180

database software is intended to store particulars of information in which elements are regularly represented by finite data and no blanks, eg every 'fish' has an individual weight and a unique tag number.

Database design generally assumes that there is obligatory uniformity in the expression of data, which is most obvious where the data are quantitative. The typical database package also accepts data in word form but often under the assumption that each expression is precise in content and finite in length, ie using the same constraints that apply with numeric data. The form of personal names tends to be regulated, eg by length, and perhaps only initials of forenames are accepted to avoid potentially lengthy entries. For some attributes the user may be obliged to select one of several options provided and by such devices data is regimented.

The most restrictive aspect of many computer database packages is the insistence that the length of every data element be specified at the outset. Novices are surprised to learn that, for computing purposes the length of all data is counted by number of characters (letters plus spaces plus punctuation), ie total number of key-strokes, and not by a count of words. A further restrictive condition is a maximum permitted length for every record, often a fixed characteristic of the software.

Of course, if curators are willing to reduce the inherent variety of information about objects to a standard set of data with limited length, a form of record could be created to facilitate handling by inflexible database systems. It would be necessary to draw up a rigid formula for recording data to be entered, something like the example (Table C). This is an extreme illustration and it is an example to be avoided. However, it emphasises the curtailment of free-text expression and the limitation of vocabulary that enable many database packages to function.

The record is broken down into numbered compartments called 'fields' and in this model every field has a fixed length. Notice that fields are of at least two types: some are reserved for determinate data, ie the options are predetermined (Table C fields 1, 4 and 7); others allow indeterminate choice but strictly limited space (fields 2,5,6 and 8) and in effect confine entries to a single term in each field or sub-field. Indeed, in those fields having predetermined options from

181

TABLE C   DATA ENTRY FORM FOR A FIXED FIELD DATABASE

1.   ACQUISITION. Check one of the following:

       a] GIFT _   b] PURCHASE _   c] AUCTION _   d] BEQUEST _

2.   RECEIVED FROM: (Name party to transaction)

       a] SURNAME ---------------   b] INITIALS ----   c] TITLE ----

3.   DATE: a] YEAR ---- b] MONTH --   c] DAY -- (numeric values only)

4.   OBJECT GROUP. Check one of the groups:

       a] MILITARY _   b] DOMESTIC _   c] INDUSTRIAL _   d] NATURAL _   e] ART

5.   OBJECT CLASS: ------------ [10 characters]

6.   ITEM NAME: --------------- [15 characters]

7.   MATERIAL: check one of,   a] TEXTILE _   b] PAPER _   c] WOOD _

                        d] STONE _   e] ORGANIC _   f] SYNTHETIC _

                        g] CERAMIC _   h] METAL, FERROUS _   i] METAL, NONFERROUS _

8.   SPECIFIC MATERIALS (limit of three):

       a] -------- , b] -------- , c] --------

9.10.11.12. etc ...   (size, age, country and town of origin, etc ...)

182

which a choice is made, the length of field is reduced to one character since the term selected can be entered by its reference code ('a', 'b' or 'c', etc). For other fields the data to be inserted is strictly limited by the measured allocation of space and in many database packages that amount of space is allocated in the computer's storage capacity, whether it be fully or only partially occupied by data or even if it remains void.

In this kind of database, if the data is variable (necessitating extravagant allocation of space to accommodate the longest entry) then many fields are under-occupied. Also if information is not always available, some fields may be void in many of the records, while holding data in only a minority. From both these causes such systems are wasteful of computer storage. It is hardly necessary to develop this case further because most curators would agree that, while single-term data and fixed-length fields have some uses in museum records, they are not able to accommodate the more variable information that is the norm in describing many attributes of collected objects. To identify a suitable software package for this kind of information on computer, we must adopt a broader definition of database.

Ignoring the self-imposed constraints of the last example, a more natural view of catalogue records reveals that most museum data are indeterminate, ie there is an indefinite number of possible answers to a standard question. An immediate illustration is the question, "Who was the maker of this object?" In the first place, we cannot assume there is only one maker to be named for each object nor can we assume that a name comprises only a single word. It can be necessary to accommodate family names of unusual length such as d'Oliveira de Albuquerque, van Borssum Waalkes, Pottier-Alapetite and Savicz-Lubitskaja.

Extending the appraisal to impersonal data, there are good reasons for not restricting descriptions to single-word responses, which always dissociate a descriptor from its subject. A phrase is more meaningful to the human mind because it expresses inter-related facts: "iron vessel with wooden handle on brass spindle" or "tempera on wood panel". Some elements are not meaningful unless they can be expressed at even greater length. In answering the question "What defects are visible on the object?", it may be necessary to record "Lower left corner lost,

183

horse's legs broken off, face of horseman damaged". Yet in many other records the same question may be answered by "none" or perhaps this field may be unoccupied by data.

Obviously, a great degree of flexibility is needed in a computer system to accommodate these variations and this is achieved by building the software on quite different lines from the fixed-field database. The main requirement is that fields should accept data of variable length and that storage space should not to be used when data is not available for a particular Element (or when that Element is inapplicable).

FREE-TEXT SEARCH

Museums whose major problem is a massive archive of records in textual form, lacking a consistent internal structure, often turn for a solution to information retrieval systems on computer that depend primarily on free-text search. That is the process by which the computer accepts any word or combination of words typed in at the keyboard to initiate a search and then retrieves all records which contain all of the matching terms. However, the results of searches of this kind can be surprising to the person making the enquiry, as retrievals can be well wide of target and sometimes they produce entirely spurious results. Several authors (eg W.M.Henry, 1984; Burton & Gates, 1985) express the view that free-text search is a strategy that demands skill and some experience on the part of the enquirer and they suggest that the method is less suitable for staff who need to make only occasional use of it. This is not intended to imply that free-text search is a flawed technique but rather to say that its success depends greatly on the content of the text to which it is applied and the skill of the enquirer.

The following assessment of its application to existing museum records assumes that the text was written without any consideration for the eventual use of computerised processing. It is for this reason that the results of free-text search may not meet initial expectations. Consider what can go wrong!

The situation in which the text was compiled without constraints on vocabulary and syntax is the worst. Even when controlled vocabulary is used, there will always be residual difficulties relating to retrieval of personal names, place-names and dates. These elements occur several times in almost every record. The reason for the difficulties that arise is that each personal name, place-name or date mentioned within a single record occurs in a particular context. Although the computer processes correctly identify every occurrence of the same name, they take no account of the adjacent context. There is no way in which the computer retrieval system can distinguish the relationship of a personal name to other data unless that relationship is established by the formal structure of the record.

Personal names occur in almost all Sections of a record: examples are seen in Statements of --- Origin: as names of maker, manufacturer, designer, artist, craftsman; --- Owners: as names of previous owners of the object; --- Association: as names of persons otherwise associated with the object; --- Discovery: as names of finder, excavator, gatherer or field-collector; --- Acquisition: names of donor, vendor, benefactor or auction house; --- Inscription: as persons named in memorial, in praise or celebration, etc; --- Imagery: as the subject of a portrait, or figured in pictorial context; --- Attribution: as author of an expert opinion or identification; --- Citation: as author of a published work, essay, review, report; --- Facsimile: when named as draughtsman, engraver, or publisher of a reproduction; etc.

From this list it is obvious that the role which a person occupies in relation to the object should be stated, if persons bearing the same name are not to be confused in retrieval by computer. Let us assume that we wish to retrieve records for all objects made in wood by a craftsman whose name is Fletcher but unfortunately we know only the initials of his fore-names 'F' and 'M'. We now discover our disadvantage for we do not know that the records contain just these initials: they could include one or both forenames in full. We must therefore search for records containing the name "Fletcher". Obviously in a large database many records will qualify, ie match this request, but few of them will refer to the man we seek. Among a wide variety of records matched we find many that are irrelevant to our enquiry, such as for objects "bequeathed by Mrs Edith Fletcher".

If we knew the craftsman's full name as Frank Morley Fletcher the retrievals would be much more specific to our requirement (but would miss records in which the name appeared as "Mr. F M Fletcher" and even "Mr. Frank M Fletcher". To succeed in retrieving all three forms of the name we would need to define them as alternatives in our search. Furthermore, in the case of records written without a structure or practical conventions, there is no certainty that the words 'craftsman' or 'wood' necessarily appear in the text: he might be described as a 'carver' or 'joiner'. In this situation we are deprived of the option of inserting just one of these terms (together with the name "Fletcher") in order to specify more closely the target of the search. Certainly it is possible to specify each of these in turn (together with the personal name) to initiate separate searches but the process becomes laborious. We also need to realise, when using 'wood' as a search term, that it may be essential actually to define the term as 'wood/////' (or by some such convention) to indicate that the retrieval should include all words of which these are the first four characters. Only by this device is it possible to extract a record containing the phrase, "woodcut by Frank Morley Fletcher after a design by J D Batten".

Let us be quite clear that, in the preceding example, the problems arising at the retrieval stage are consequences derived from two rather distinct conditions. One is the universal problem of synonymy, which is manifested here in a multi-word phrase (a 'character-string' including spaces): "Frank Morley Fletcher" and "Frank M Fletcher" are synonyms, as also is "(Mr.) F M Fletcher". The other condition affecting the incidence of personal names in free-text is the necessity of identifying their functional context, ie our search is for F M Fletcher, craftsman, as distinct from others of that name who might be publisher or benefactor. The risk of indiscriminate retrieval is obviously greater in the case of commoner surnames, such as Brown, Jones, and Smith as any telephone directory will confirm. Unless certain terms serving as role-indicators are included together with the names of persons mentioned in a textual record, the proportion of target records retrieved in response to a request in which the search term is a personal name will be less than 100% and can often be unacceptably low.

An analogous situation arises in the case of retrievals based on place-names; not because there are so many places with identical names, but because the names of places are cited in so many differing contexts. Place-names can occur in the following Sections of any record, Location: the place where a museum object is stored or exhibited (eg store depot, branch museum or out-station); Origin: as the place where the object was made; Discovery: where the object was excavated or found; under Imagery: as names of places represented in any kind of image; also in Derivation: any place mentioned in describing an artistic source; in Association: places recording historical events or former location of an object; Exhibition: places where an object has been exhibited; and finally in Citation: as place of publication.

There is even the possibility that identical names relating to both persons and places may result in the retrieval of irrelevant records. Assuming that we wish to retrieve records for all objects that were made in the town of Reading, the search may be defined by the two keywords 'manufacture(d)' and 'Reading'. In the absence of additional geographic data (often omitted from the original text), eg the county name, there is no way in which we can more closely define our request to ensure selective retrieval. The records retrieved logically include Example 34, which appears to be totally inappropriate because it refers to a desk manufactured not in Reading but in Birmingham! The infallible logic of the computer, matching the criteria for selection, has identified this record because it includes both of the required keywords: 'Reading' is the surname of a woman and the other, 'manufacture(r)', is a description of her father's occupation.

Example 34   Writing Desk c.1866

> Rectangular form, 15 x 9½ x 6 inches, inlaid with mother of pearl; silver shield fixed to top and engraved "H READING". Given by Charles Lyster to his daughter Hannah Reading on occasion of her wedding. Lyster was a specialist tortoiseshell and pearl manufacturer at 22, 24, 26 and 28 Spencer Street, Birmingham. Bequeathed by Mrs. Edith Fletcher, daughter of Mrs Hannah Reading.

Some free-text retrieval packages have a facility (called 'proximity searching') allowing an enquirer to specify in the search parameters that the required keywords must occur within (say) 5 contiguous words of text (the exact number is variable at will). Naturally, this can overcome some of the apparent disadvantages just mentioned but it should be noted that its benefits only apply where the original text was constructed within a disciplined framework. The essence of the requirement is to be confident that, in all records, the place-name element occurs within a phrase of (let us say) 5 words which also includes the role-indicator, eg 'published', 'manufactured' (or whatever it may be).

Retrieval of dates is unlikely to be successful in free-text because they occur in so many different contexts, eg

Example 35   John Dickson Batten (1860-1932), "Eve and the Serpent". Colour woodcut, exhibited Birmingham Art Gallery, in an Exhibition of English Woodcut Colour Prints, April-May 1940. A footnote on p.48 of "A History of Woodcut" by A M Hind (Vol. 1) 1935, states: "Eve and the Serpent, cut by Frank Morley Fletcher after a design by J D Batten, proved 1895 and published 1896, is among the earliest English prints in the Japanese method." Purchased 1940.

This record contains six different dates, one of which repeats in two different contexts. Suppose that it was desired to retrieve records for all woodcuts dating from 1940 and later years: Example 35 would be included in the result of a search (based on the keywords 'woodcut' and '1940'). In fact "Eve and the Serpent" was exhibited in that year, and purchased in that year, but it was created 45 years earlier (the artist died in 1932). How can these three events be separated and related to their respective dates? Let's look at the operation of the facility (already described) which prescribes that both keywords in this search should occur within a string of 5 consecutive words, inferring a relational connection between them. Using the same record, we find that searches for the keywords 'proved' and 'published' retrieve this record when either term is paired with year 1895 and again with 1896, but in each case only one date is actually correct. However, a search

188

for keyword 'exhibited' combined with date '1940' would <u>not</u> retrieve this record under the five-word proximity condition. In the original text, 'exhibited' is the function-defining term and is the leading term in its statement, followed by venue, then by title of the exhibition and lastly its date. If a convention applied to ensure that the date was stated directly after the function ('exhibited') then retrieval under these rules would succeed.

<u>Example 36</u>   Royal Artillery Dress Sword and Scabbard. English. Steel blade, engraved with scrolls, the arms, crest and motto of the R.A. Inscribed with maker's name and place of manufacture; "E. Thurkle, 5 Denmark Street, Soho, London." Scabbard of steel, covering of American cloth.

This provides another illustration of indiscriminate retrieval when using free-text search methods, arising from the occurrence of several geographical names within an individual record. In this case, the record contains names referring to three different nations: 'English','American' and 'Denmark'. There is no way for a free-text retrieval system to relate these names to their respective context unless some kind of structure is introduced when compiling the record. This record (as shown) will answer a geographical query relating to any one of those countries.

If the record is divided into several paragraphs (to match with the Sections of REFORM), we can isolate details of maker's name and place of manufacture, ie "E. Thurkle, 5 Denmark Street, Soho, London". Directing the search for country name to this statement alone, the record qualifies for retrieval on the word 'Denmark' (intentionally requesting articles made in that country) when in fact the country of origin is England. It is not retrievable on a search for 'England' due to omission of that term from the original statement. It can be seen, therefore, that even by dividing records into paragraphs and targeting them separately for search, retrievals cannot be guaranteed to meet expectations if the writing of statements is unregulated. It can be argued that this example represents a small minority of records, in which several national titles occur in disparate contexts. Nevertheless,

189

it is clearly desirable either to establish some conventions on content of textual statements or to supplement records in free-text with classified headings, for example, using Elements from REFORM Section 2.2.0. Because these Elements demand consistency in the terms applied to concepts such as period, century, country, province, object type, etc. enquiry using recognised search terms succeeds in retrieving relevant data.

DISCUSSING THE OPTIONS

In a useful review naming some of the well-known data management software for information storage and retrieval, Roberts (1985, sections C2.8; 2.9) mentions among the problems relating to them, their lack of portability between different types of machine. While this is often true in a strict sense (in that software cannot simply be unloaded from one maker's machine and transferred to another) many of these packages are available on as many as five or six models of computer from more than one manufacturer. What is perhaps a more serious omission is his failure to mention packages developed on the UNIX, UCSD (p-system) and PICK operating systems which are portable and which offer freedom of choice in hardware.

The GOS package, to which the Museum Documentation Association harnessed its entire data-processing facility, is acknowledged to be unable to provide rapid general information retrieval (ie on-line), and according to Roberts (1985) "has restricted overall retrieval capabilities" in comparison with many other systems and "limited facilities for up-dating records". This means it is a non-contender as a vehicle for collection management.

If careful thought is given to preparing text with the intention of using a free-text retrieval method, it is capable of serving the purpose to good effect but if this method is to be applied to existing text, some time and effort must be given to revising its content with the aid of a word-processing package.

It can be seen from the preceding discussion that neither normal database nor the free-text retrieval system alone is ideally suited for museum records. The need seems to be for a system that incorporates

190

the best features of both without the limitations of either of them! To be realistic, we must concede that this perfectionist prescription is probably unattainable but there is still much to be gained from a determined attempt to combine the best features in a single package. Beware of any advice that suggests the museum's records are of two types (fixed length and variable length, or 'factual' and 'conceptual') and that a separate software package is required for each (Townley, 1978). Such a proposition is a recipe for disaster because the only link between the two halves of every record split in this way may be the object's accession number. Enquiries must then be duplicated and data that are accessed separately cannot be combined into a single report.

What are the desirable features of information systems equipped to satisfy the varied requirements of curatorship and collection management? The ability of the system to accept elements of variable length is certainly essential: to choose otherwise (by adopting a database system with fixed length fields) is to adopt unnecessary restrictions. The fact that some Elements in museum records are of a formal character, and therefore are themselves defined in length, is no obstacle to their use in systems that do not require such definition. When using systems in which field lengths are unspecified and variable, it is only necessary to calculate total storage requirements from the average length of record or element. This average value can be obtained easily from inspection of the largest, the smallest and the most frequent (modal) lengths of data in a sample of records. This method allows for variable data to be accommodated in computer systems where storage is allocated and taken up as data are fed in.

When considering what is demanded of a museum information system the conclusion is reached that it must give rapid access to -- and retrieval of -- relevant information. For most purposes a more precise definition of "relevant information" could be expressed as "desired elements of information". This is the clue to a versatile computer-based system of record management. If what we generally require is to recall selected facts about objects, it is logical to choose a system that operates by storing and retrieving Statements and /or Elements, rather than unitary records. From experience of dissecting text records (Chapter 3)

191

through the analytical use of REFORM, we recognise that records can be considered as chains of Statements (these being chains of Elements) connected basically because they refer to the same object. What is needed, therefore, in a computer system for structured information is the facility to treat records as logical rather than as physical entities.

Typical database systems hold all the data for each record in one "parking lot" and locate it on request by reference to its "street - address". Conventionally the sequence in which records are stored (by analogy with automobiles) is the order of arrival in the "parking lot" and, therefore, to locate a friend's car you would need to know at what time it checked-in. To find the same vehicle by reference to the name of the car's owner would require an index but in museum records a single index is hardly sufficient. Museum work involves concurrent use of several index files through which requests for data retrieval can be directed to the relevant records. Each index typically includes one line for every data record in the main file and so every index contains as many entries as the file itself. There is, however, an alternative strategy for locating and gaining access to records on computer.

The critical feature that is necessary in order to maximise the word-retrieval capability of the system is the indexing method known as 'inverted file' organisation. In text-retrieval and document-retrieval systems this is the usual search technique as it short-circuits the need to read the whole body of text in locating the occurrence of particular words. It is typically employed to index the entire text of a document. Museum catalogues can use the same technique to deliver only those facts selected as being relevant to enquiry by creating inverted files for each Section (when treated as textual paragraphs) or for particular Elements (when structured at this level).

Reverting to our automobile analogy, the 'inverted file' is a list of all the tyre sizes (and other components) for all the vehicles in our area and, for each size of tyre, it includes the "phone number" for every depot holding that item in store. Thus it is not merely an index to tyre depots (which leaves further enquiries to be made) but in effect it is the combined stock-list of those depots. In general terms, an inverted list is not simply a directory to all occurrences of an Element

192

holding data of one kind (eg tyre size as a category) but it is a check-list of the actual data (eg every tyre size in numeric values). The method operates with equal effect where each 'value' is a word taken from a textual expression, whether constructed as formal or free text. This method results in much shorter response time for data-retrieval in conjunctive searches (when two or more attributes are sought with specified values of each) than is possible with standard indexes.

The advantages of inverted file systems are most evident when the record revision rate (ie frequency of data amendment) is low relative to the enquiry rate (ie frequency of data retrieval) (Claybrook, 1983). Referring to a previous comparison, it is less appropriate, therefore, for a theatre or airline reservation system where almost every enquiry results in amendment (to the number and location of seats remaining available) but it is exactly suited to the situation found in museum record systems. Here a majority of searches are performed for the purpose of retrieving information without need to amend it: access to elements for amendment is infrequent relative to all retrievals and amendment of one element only rarely modifies another.

Those database management systems that are suitable for handling an information resource as complex as museum catalogues must possess a feature known in computer terms as a data dictionary. Contrary to first impressions, this does not mean a list of word definitions but instead it implies a facility for defining data structures like REFORM. With this feature a computer system can be programmed to group Statements using templates tailored to the needs of particular museum collections. We cannot pretend that the structured form of record for a watch (Example 3) will be the same as that for a woodcut (Example 35). Of course, there are broad similarities between such records (as we have emphasized throughout this book) but within the envelope of similarity there are selective differences affecting inclusion or exclusion of certain Statements and Elements. Examples of the appropriate selections for various thematic collections are given in Appendix II. The point now under consideration is how such templates for structured information can be implemented on computer. The answer to that question is to invoke the facilities of 'dictionary driven' software systems.

To clarify the implications we must return to the conceptual framework of REFORM. The Statements are filed in Sections, notionally represented as file-boxes: therefore the contents of any Section can be regarded as a 'file'. This is a fundamental unit of computerised data-handling and all files must be defined in the dictionary facility. Now it is apparent that, for any museum object, we need to create a Statement in the Acquisition File (ie Section), a Statement in the Identity File, another in the Origin File, another in the Description File, and so on; the list of files included depending on the type of collection to which the object belongs. In computer language the museum 'record' for one object is translated as a group of related records spread among various files. The curator should therefore think of the catalogue of (let us say) folk-life crafts or scientific instruments, as comprising a separate 'database', ie an entity at a higher level than a file. A database incorporates data that is stored for convenience in several files.

The importance of the dictionary facility now becomes clearer: it enables the user to define a database for each major type of collection by reference to a common set of building blocks (ie REFORM Sections), making an appropriate selection from those available to accommodate the peculiarities of the information relating to collections of that type. Furthermore, the data dictionary makes it possible to extract required information across several databases because the temporary joining of databases is accomplished within such computer systems while a search is conducted.

Without data dictionary facilities a database package is more truly described as a file-handler and its possibilities are more limited. For example, each collection might require a separate file incorporating many Sections of REFORM and consequently including an excessive number of Elements (data 'fields'). In this situation every field must be newly defined for every file in which it is used, while under a data dictionary facility each field is defined just once. This ensures consistency throughout the information system and also saves much programming effort. Without a data dictionary it is unlikely that file definitions can be modified after they have been set up and data has been entered.

Another characteristic that is essential to the full exploitation of REFORM, and which is more usually found in dictionary-driven systems, is the facility to accept multi-value fields. This means simply that an Element is allowed to repeat within a record so that, for example in a Statement of Origin, we can insert into appropriate Elements all of the following data referring to the origin of one object:

"artist"   (1.4.2) .... Bertini, Piero (1.4.1)

"engraver" (1.4.2) .... Dupont, Marcel (1.4.1)

"printer"   (1.4.2) ..... Volesque et Cie (1.4.1)

For an engraving it is necessary to record all the above names and their respective roles in the Statement of Origin since all three persons contributed to its creation. The personal names are held in one Element (1.4.1) and the role descriptors are held in another (1.4.2): both of them must link and repeat as many times as there are roles to describe. Repeating fields are necessary to accommodate, for example, Elements 1.1.5; 1.2.1; 1.3.1; 1.4.1; 1.6.1; 3.2.1 and possibly others. For some situations multi-value fields are needed to accept alternative names (an 'alias') for a single object or association (see example under 1.3.1).

Additional benefits of a dictionary-driven system include the option of introducing alternative names for every Element (field) in a file, enabling the computer to recognise retrieval requests made by curators who prefer to use the vocabulary of their own discipline. Thus, a curator of Archaeology refers to the place of excavation as a 'Site', while in Natural History the place in which the specimen was collected is called a 'Locality'. Both terms relate to data stored in Element 1.6.4 which names the findspot and the computer can accept both terms in commands designed to retrieve relevant information, eg "list name of finder, site and date" (Archaeology); and "list name of finder, locality and date" (Nat. Hist). A curator of Industrial History refers to the place where an object was made as a 'Factory' while Art curators use the word 'Atelier' for equivalent information about a picture/print. Both are related by a computer dictionary to data held in Element 1.4.4. The fact that these names are aliases can remain unknown to the respective users of such a system, who are presented by the computer screen with only the terminology appropriate to their own academic discipline.

195

CONCLUSION

One thing is certain where computerisation is concerned: competing attractions of different machines and of rival software have already killed the unlikely prospect that any single computer package might become the universal vehicle for museum systems. Indeed, that would be contrary to common experience in many other professional fields such as architectural design, legal and library documentation, medical records and financial management. In every one of these fields there are alternative methods of computerised processing, all of which achieve the desired objectives. In the field of museum documentation, therefore, software systems are needed that can be adopted under differing local circumstances and which offer features suited to the museum's data.

From the preceding exploration of facilities that are available for database operation on minicomputers, even on some personal computers, it is clear that software can be found to process museum records if the choice is carefully considered. The necessary software consists of an operating system which serves to harness the machinery and a text-oriented data storage and retrieval system (see: Hamilton et al., 1985). Ideally the latter will include a data dictionary, data security features, a natural query language and ancillary tools for screen and report formatting. The standard package does not possess any 'interface' features specific to museum requirements, ie wording of screen displays, prompts to the user, names of files, guides to interrogation of the database, etc. Using the facilities of an 'application generator', these can be produced by a member of museum staff who has received a period of training on a range of courses, for example, as provided by the National Computing Centre (NCC). However, many museums find they cannot spare a member of staff from normal duties for computer training and managers often take the view that the costs of training might be better spent on purchasing a package in which the raw system is completely customized before acceptance (the so-called 'turn-key' option). This work can only be done by consultants who specialise in the field of bibliographic and museological databases, who advise on the software to meet the purpose and customise it to match specific preferences, leaving the purchaser with a system ready to run.

The methods of transferring archival records to any computer system rank equally with the choice of software in determining the success or failure of the project because the demands placed upon museum staff are dependent on the method adopted. In simple terms, if a conventional database package is (unwisely) chosen, the consequence is likely to involve curators in the mammoth task of rewriting archival records into a strictly structured form before any attempt to input the data is possible. This way there is a double penalty to pay: firstly, heavy demands are placed on curatorial time for a task that is slow and intellectually intensive; secondly, keyboard operators are required to read and type from manuscript documents of uneven legibility or from detailed forms of great complexity. Avoidance of the task of re-writing extensive data is probably the most important part of the strategy for computerising archives.

One means of transferring archival data to computer by an automated method is to use the services of an agency that offers data capture by optical character recognition (OCR). The optical character reader is a device for scanning typed or printed documents and for converting the individual characters into digital signals for storage on magnetic tape, which can then be 'read' by computer. The limitation of this technique is that the scanner must be programmed to recognise the characters of a particular size and font. Problems arise if there are changes of font within a document or paragraph. It is most useful where the archival data to be transferred are found in a single source document, eg one catalogue card for each object, but less useful if there are data in several separate documentary systems relating to all objects. The method is not applicable to records typed in unusual type-faces unless special programming is undertaken: obviously it is useless for handwritten data.

If the condition of archival records does not permit transcription by OCR, then the best alternative is to use bureau services for what is called 'data preparation' or 'keying'. This involves sending batches of catalogue cards or document sheets to a bureau where skilled keyboard operators type from the original direct to computer, producing magnetic tape ready for loading into the museum's computer. External 'data-prep' bureaux can devote perhaps as many as fifty keyboard staff to the job and their operatives are trained in high-speed work, with the result that a rapid turn-round of processed data can be achieved.

On receiving the prepared tape, a museum can devote the efforts of its own staff to editing the unimproved records into shape compatible with the REFORM structure. This editing is performed at the computer screen (not by pencil and paper) and can be placed in the hands of competent keyboard staff after preliminary briefing and some training. This leaves the curator with the supervisory role, monitoring progress and checking output. The merits of REFORM in this process are that every data Element that is recognised by the operative in the original text of a record can be given a mark of identification by inserting its Element number as prefix and another keystroke to signal its termination. Editing by this on-screen technique produces a new version of every record punctuated by REFORM numbers which act as signals to the computer to assign those data to the fields designated for them by the data dictionary. By this procedure archival records are converted into structured records compatible with REFORM and capable of being selected, sequenced and retrieved as desired. Databases compiled in this form have the potential to serve as on-line catalogues, to print lists and reports and to maintain up-to-date records for the practical management of collections.

———————————

REFERENCES

Ashford, J.H. (1984) "Storage and Retrieval of Bibliographic Records: comparison of database management systems and free text approaches. Program vol.18 no.1 (Jan.) p.16-45.

Ashford, J.H. and D.I. Matkin (1982) "Studies on the Application of Free Text Package Systems" London: Clive Bingley and The Library Association. 50pp.

Boyce, Cheryl (1982) 'MINISIS' (a relational information system) Program vol.16 no.3 (July) p.131-141.

Brooks, C.H.P., P.J.Grouse, D.R.Jeffery and M.J.Lawrence (1982) "Information Systems Design" Sydney: Prentice-Hall 477p.

Burton, P.F. and H.Gates (1985) "Library software for microcomputers" Program vol.19 no.1 (Jan.) p.1-19.

Claybrook, Billy G. (1983) "File Management Techniques" New York: Chichester: Brisbane: John Wiley & Sons 247pp. (technical account of inverted file and other index methods in terms of computer functions)

Croft, W.B. (1982) "An Overview of Information Systems" Information Technology: Research and Development no.1 p.73-96.

Elbra, Tony (1982) "Database for the small computer user" Manchester, England: National Computing Centre Ltd. (useful definitions and understandable explanations: compares IBM System 38 and CMC Reality System)

Hamilton, C.D., R.Kimberley and C.H.Smith (1985) "Text Retrieval: a Directory of Software" Aldershot (UK); Brookfield, VT(USA): Gower Publishing Company, with the Institute of Information Scientists. Also with above title: 1985/86 Supplement ed. Kimberley.

Henry, W.M. (1984) "Viewdata-type searching in a free-text system..." Program vol.18 no.4 (Oct.) p.308-320.

199

Kurtz, L.A. (1984) "An Introduction to Database Management Systems" Program vol.18 no.1 (Jan.) p.1-15.

Roberts, D.A.(1985) "Planning the Documentation of Museum Collections" Duxford, Cambridge: Museum Documentation Association. 568 pp.

Smither, R. (1985) "... transferring the documentation of the Imperial War Museum's film collection." MDA Information vol 9, no 3, p.67-74.

Smither, R.B.N. (1986) "The Imperial War Museum", Chapter 14 in Museum Documentation Systems ... edited by R.B.Light, D.A.Roberts and J.D.Stewart. Butterworths.

Sarasan, L. and A.M.Neuner (1983) "Museum Collections and Computers" Lawrence, Kansas: Association of Systematics Collections. 292pp.

Tagg, R.M. (1982) "Bibliographic and commercial databases: contrasting approaches to data management with special reference to DBMS". Program vol.16 no.4 (Oct.) p.191-199.

Townley, H.M. (1978) "Systems Analysis for Information Retrieval" London: Andre Deutsch, in association with the Institute of Information Scientists. 120pp.

Wilson, P.A. (1986) "Introducing Electronic Filing" 154pp. Manchester, England: National Computing Centre Ltd.

Program is published by Aslib, the Association for Information Management, 26-27 Boswell Street, London WC1 N 3JZ.

Appendix I

Rapid reference to data elements

The following pages provide a method of rapid reference to the Elements that comprise the comprehensive museum record system REFORM. Individual Elements of information that contribute to a record can be readily identified from the appropriate questions in the listings below.

Simply read down the list until you encounter the question on which you require further information or guidance; then consult the paragraph of the same number to be found in Chapters 7,8,9,10 in numerical order.

The arrangement of the questions in this Appendix cuts across the thematic arrangement by Sections employed in the main text of the book. This may make it easier to find the Element required because there are just five simple lists with no special structure or hierarchy.

Part (1)   lists data Elements concerned with 'THINGS',
           (not merely the objects themselves but all aspects that can be
           described in answer to the question "What ...?")

Part (2)   lists data Elements concerned with aspects of METHOD, process,
           purpose and role (responses to the question "How ...")

Part (3)   lists data Elements concerned with PERSONS involved in any way
           (past or present) with a museum object (answering the question
           "Who ...?")

Part (4)   lists data Elements concerned with all references to PLACE,
           site and position, both on the object itself and in the world
           at large (answers to the question "Where ...?")

Part (5)   lists data Elements concerned with all references to TIME,
           both as dates of varying precision and as descriptive terms
           for intervals of any duration (answering the question "When?")

part (1)

DATA RELATING TO OBJECTS AND THEIR ATTRIBUTES

What is the museum's identity number for this object?	2.1.1
What is the title (if any) of this work?	2.1.4
What is the name of the design, model or series?	2.1.4
What is the denomination of the coin?	2.1.4
What is the brief description of the object?	2.1.5
What is the expert opinion of this object?	3.2.4
What is the previous identity number/ lot number?	2.1.7
What is the serial number of the article?	2.1.7
What is the excavator's number for this object?	2.1.7
What is the class name for this type of object? (exact group)	2.2.9
To which broader category does it belong?	2.2.8
To which general series of objects does it belong?	2.2.7
What culture or style is the object associated with?	1.3.7
What is the detailed description of the object?	2.3.1
What part of the object is described (if not the whole)?	2.3.2
What is /are the material(s) of which it is made?	2.3.3
What is the form /shape of the article or specimen?	2.3.4
What kind of surface decoration is present?	2.3.5
What measurements were made of the object? (give dimensions)	2.3.6
What is the gender and age of sitter/wearer? (portrait/costume)	2.3.7
What is the gender and life-stage of the specimen? (animal)	2.3.7
What other objects belong to the same suite?	1.3.6
What type of signatory marks are visible on the object?	2.4.1
What are the maker's marks, hall/assay marks, signatures?	2.4.4
What interpretation can be made of these?	2.4.5
What object/work of art inspired the making of this object?	1.5.1
What objects/animals/inanimate things are depicted?	2.6.2
What activities or events are depicted?	2.6.6
What is the thematic description of the image?	2.6.7
What is the inscription on the object?	2.5.1
What is the translation of the inscription?	2.5.2
In which language is the inscription made?	2.5.3
What is the title of the exhibition in which object was shown?	3.3.2
What is the title of the publication cited?	3.4.2
What is the title of the reproduction/facsimile?	3.5.5
What is the type status of the specimen?	4.1.1
What is the physical condition of the object?	4.1.1
What are the physical defects of the object?	4.1.3
What price was paid on purchase of the object?	1.1.4
What sum was received by grant towards the purchase?	1.1.6
What sum was received on disposal of the object by sale?	4.1.7
What is the assessed value of the object?	4.2.1
What is the insurance schedule number covering the object?	4.2.4
What part(s) of the object is /are being loaned?	4.4.1

202

Part (2)

DATA RELATING TO METHOD, PROCESS, PURPOSE, ROLE

How was the object acquired by the museum?	1.1.2
What special conditions were imposed on its acquisition?	1.1.8
How did the previous owner acquire possession of the object?	1.2.2
What was the role of the person named in creating the object?	1.4.2
What was the process /technique used in its manufacture?	1.4.3
What was the role of the person named in its discovery?	1.6.2
In what trade, industry or general context was it used?	1.7.1
In what process or activity was it used?	1.7.2
What was the object's precise function?	1.7.3
How was it used /handled?	1.7.4
What museum role /function is the object best suited for?	4.1.2
What is the conceptual role /purpose of the image?	2.6.1
What method was used to apply his mark by the maker?	2.4.3
What method was used to apply the inscription?	2.5.4
What method of examination /investigation was used?	3.1.4
What method of conservation treatment was used?	3.1.5
What chemical reagents were used in its conservation?	3.1.6
How was the object involved in the named historical event?	1.3.5
In what medium or method is the expert opinion given?	3.2.5
What function does the cited publication serve?	3.4.6
What process was used to create the facsimile /reproduction?	3.5.4
What is the purpose for which the object is being loaned?	4.4.4
What special conditions were made by museum on its disposal?	4.1.8
How was the object disposed of /written off?	4.1.5

Part (3)

DATA RELATING TO PERSONS

What is the name of the vendor /donor /testator /auction house?	1.1.1
Who was the first /subsequent /latest owner of the object?	1.2.1
To whom did the above owner transfer possession?	1.2.5
From whom did the above owner obtain possession?	1.2.5
Who is associated with the object by historical circumstance?	1.3.1
What organisation /body was the object associated with?	1.3.1
Who was the maker /designer /creator of the object?	1.4.1
Who was the draughtsman /engraver? (if object is a print)	1.4.1
Who was the issuing authority (coins)?	1.4.1
Who was the finder /excavator of the object?	1.6.1
Who was the user /operator of the object when functioning?	1.7.8
Who created the precursor which inspired this object?	1.5.3
Who produced the print derived from it? (object is a picture)	3.5.1
Who is the person depicted in the portrait /image?	2.6.3
Who made the cast /reproduction of this object?	3.5.1
Who was the publisher?	3.4.3
Who is responsible for the information given in this record?	2.1.6
What is the name of conservator/institute treating the object?	3.1.2
What is the name of curator submitting object for conservation?	3.1.3
What is the name of the person/institute exhibiting the object?	3.3.3
What is the name of the expert giving opinion on attribution?	3.2.1
Who is the author of the published work cited?	3.4.1
Who was the recipient? (if object was disposed of by sale)	4.1.6
Who authorised its disposal /certified its loss?	4.1.9
Who assessed the insurance value of the object?	4.2.2
What is the name of the borrower /lender of the object?	4.4.2
What is the name of the source of grant aid?	1.1.5
What is the name of the department curating the object?	2.1.2

Part (4)

DATA RELATING TO PLACE, POSITION, SITE

What is the address of the vendor /donor /auction house?	1.1.3
What is the address of the borrower /lender?	4.4.3
What is the address /official role/ of the expert referee?	3.2.2
Where was the object kept by its former owner?	1.2.3
Where was the object used (location) when functioning?	1.7.6
Which place is historically associated with the object?	1.3.3
Where was the object made /created /manufactured?	1.4.4
Where is /was the precursor that inspired the present work?	1.5.2
Where was the object discovered /excavated /captured?	1.6.4
What are the geographical co-ordinates of the find-spot?	1.6.5
In what environment /habitat /rock-unit was the object found?	1.6.6
In which local geographical district is the discovery site?	2.2.3
In which broader geographical area is this district situated?	2.2.2
In which global geographical division is it classed?	2.2.1
Which place /district is depicted? (pictorial image)	2.6.4
Where on the object is the maker's mark?	2.4.2
Where on the object is the inscription positioned?	2.5.5
What part /area of the object was treated /conserved?	3.1.7
Where was the cited reference published?	3.4.5
Where is the facsimile /replica of this object?	3.5.2
Where was the object exhibited? (city /address)	3.3.4
Where is the object normally exhibited /stored?	4.3.1
What is its exact position in that location? (case, shelf)	4.3.2
Where is the object temporarily located?	4.3.4

Part (5)

DATA RELATING TO TIME, PERIOD, DATE

What was the date when the object was acquired?	1.1.7
When did the previous owner possess the object? (from .. to)	1.2.4
What historical occasion /event is the item associated with?	1.3.2
When did that historical event occur?	1.3.4
What period is depicted in historical representation? (image)	2.6.5
When was the object made /produced /created?	1.4.5
If object derives from a precursor, when was that made?	1.5.4
When was the object found /excavated /captured?	1.6.3
In what circumstances /events was the object used?	1.7.5
At what date was the object used /in operation /functioning?	1.7.7
What century /millenium does the object date from?	2.2.6
What named period does the object date from?	2.2.5
What major era /time interval is the object classed under?	2.2.4
What is the date on which this record was made?	2.1.3
What date was the conservation work completed?	3.1.1
What date was the conservation work requested?	3.1.8
What date was the conservation work started?	3.1.9
What is the date of the expert opinion?	3.2.3
What was the date of the exhibition?	3.3.1
When was the cited article published?	3.4.4
When was the reproduction of the object made?	3.5.3
When was the status /condition report last amended?	4.1.4
When was the latest valuation made?	4.2.3
When was the object transferred to new location?	4.3.3
How long is the period of loan? (prefix OUT/ or IN)	4.4.5
When is the object due for dispatch (OUT) /or arrival (IN)?	4.4.6
When is the loan object due for return?	4.4.7
What date was the loan actually returned?	4.4.8

Appendix II

Data elements for thematic collections

The following templates represent the categories of information most likely to be used in devising records for Collections of the type named in the heading to each plan. A standard tabular arrangement facilitates comparison from one to the next. The names of Sections are stated and beneath each of them, as applicable, the reference numbers of relevant Elements are found.

The list of Elements needed in some Sections extends up to nine in total but for convenience in presentation, listing of the complete set is indicated by 'etc.'. Absence of this abbreviation means that only those Elements actually referenced are required. Not every Section is mandatory and an appropriate selection from those included can be made to suit the particular purposes of the record system.

(1) TEMPLATE of data elements for <u>PICTURES & OTHER IMAGERY</u>

STATUS 4.1.1 4.1.2 4.1.3 etc.	**VALUATION** 4.2.1 4.2.2 4.2.3 4.2.4	**LOCATION** 4.3.1 4.3.2 4.3.3 4.3.4	**LOAN** 4.4.1 4.4.2 4.4.3 etc.	/./.	/./.
CONSERVAT'N 3.1.1 3.1.2 3.1.3 etc.	**ATTRIBUTION** 3.2.1 3.2.2 3.2.3 3.2.4	**EXHIBITION** 3.3.1 3.3.2 3.3.3 3.3.4	**CITATION** 3.4.1 3.4.2 3.4.3 etc.	**FACSIMILE** 3.5.1 3.5.2 3.5.3 etc.	/./.
IDENTITY 2.1.1 2.1.2 2.1.3 etc.	**CLASSIFIC'N** 2.2.4 2.2.5 2.2.6	**DESCRIPTION** 2.3.2 2.3.3 2.3.6	**MAKER'S MARK** 2.4.1 2.4.2 2.4.3 etc.	**INSCRIPTION** 2.5.1 2.5.2 2.5.3 etc.	**IMAGERY** 2.6.1 2.6.2 2.6.3 etc.
ACQUISITION 1.1.1 1.1.2 1.1.3 etc.	**OWNERSHIP** 1.2.1 1.2.2 1.2.3 etc.	**ASSOCIATION**	**ORIGIN** 1.4.1 1.4.2 1.4.3 etc.	**DERIVATION** 1.5.1 1.5.2 1.5.3 etc.	**DISCOVERY**

(2) TEMPLATE of data elements for <u>COSTUME COLLECTIONS</u>

STATUS	VALUATION	LOCATION	LOAN	/./.	/./.
4.1.1	4.2.1	4.3.1	4.4.1		
4.1.2	4.2.2	4.3.2	4.4.2		
4.1.3	4.2.3	4.3.3	4.4.3		
etc.	4.2.4	4.3.4	etc.	/./.	/./.

CONSERVAT'N	ATTRIBUTION	EXHIBITION	CITATION	FACSIMILE	/./.
3.1.1		3.3.1	3.4.1		
3.1.2		3.3.2	3.4.2		
3.1.3		3.3.3	3.4.3		
etc.		3.3.4	etc.		/./.

IDENTITY	CLASSIFIC'N	DESCRIPTION	MAKER'S MARK	INSCRIPTION	IMAGERY
2.1.1	2.2.1	2.3.3	2.4.1		
2.1.2	2.2.2	2.3.6	2.4.2		
2.1.3	2.2.3	2.3.7	2.4.3		
etc.	etc.		etc.		

ACQUISITION	OWNERSHIP	ASSOCIATION	ORIGIN	DERIVATION	DISCOVERY
1.1.1	1.2.1	1.3.1	1.4.1		
1.1.2	1.2.2	1.3.2	1.4.2		
1.1.3	1.2.3	1.3.3	1.4.3		
etc.	etc.	etc.	etc.		

209

(3) TEMPLATE of data elements for ARCHAEOLOGY & ETHNOGRAPHY

STATUS	VALUATION	LOCATION	LOAN	
4.1.1	4.2.1	4.3.1	4.4.1	/././
4.1.2	4.2.2	4.3.2	4.4.2	
4.1.3	4.2.3	4.3.3	4.4.3	
etc.	4.2.4	4.3.4	etc.	/././

CONSERVAT'N	ATTRIBUTION	EXHIBITION	CITATION	FACSIMILE
3.1.1	3.2.1		3.4.1	/././
3.1.2	3.2.2		3.4.2	
3.1.3	3.2.3		3.4.3	
etc.	3.2.4		etc.	/././

IDENTITY	CLASSIFIC'N	DESCRIPTION	MAKER'S MARK	INSCRIPTION	IMAGERY	
2.1.1	2.2.1	2.3.1	2.4.1	2.5.1	2.6.1	
2.1.2	2.2.2	2.3.2	2.4.2	2.5.2	2.6.2	/././
2.1.3	2.2.3	2.3.3	2.4.3	2.5.3	2.6.3	
etc.	to 2.2.6	to 2.3.6	etc.	etc.	etc.	/././

ACQUISITION	OWNERSHIP	ASSOCIATION	ORIGIN	DERIVATION	DISCOVERY	FUNCTION
1.1.1	1.2.1		1.4.1		1.6.1	1.7.1
1.1.2	1.2.2				1.6.2	1.7.2
1.1.3	1.2.3	1.3.7	1.4.3		1.6.3	1.7.3
etc.	etc.				etc.	etc.

(4) TEMPLATE of data elements for MANUFACTURES /CERAMIC /METAL etc

STATUS	VALUATION	LOCATION	LOAN	/./.	/./.	
4.1.1	4.2.1	4.3.1	4.4.1			
4.1.2	4.2.2	4.3.2	4.4.2			
4.1.3	4.2.3	4.3.3	4.4.3			
etc.	4.2.4	4.3.4	etc.			
CONSERVAT'N	**ATTRIBUTION** /./.	**EXHIBITION** /./.	**CITATION**	**FACSIMILE** /./.		
3.1.1			3.4.1			
3.1.2			3.4.2			
3.1.3			3.4.3			
etc.			etc.			
IDENTITY	**CLASSIFIC'N**	**DESCRIPTION**	**MAKER'S MARK**	**INSCRIPTION**	**IMAGERY** /./.	
2.1.1	2.2.4	2.3.1	2.4.1	2.5.1		
2.1.2	2.2.5	2.3.2	2.4.2	2.5.2		
2.1.3	2.2.6	2.3.3	2.4.3	2.5.3		
etc.	to 2.2.9	2.3.6	etc.	etc.		
ACQUISITION	**OWNERSHIP**	**ORIGIN**	**ASSOCIATION**	**DERIVATION**	**DISCOVERY**	**FUNCTION**
1.1.1	1.2.1	1.4.1				1.7.1
1.1.2	1.2.2	1.4.2				1.7.2
1.1.3	1.2.3	1.4.3				1.7.3
etc.	etc.	etc.				etc.

211

APPENDIX [II]

(5) TEMPLATE of data elements for LOCAL HISTORY /FOLK-LIFE

STATUS	VALUATION	LOCATION	LOAN		
4.1.1	4.2.1	4.3.1	4.4.1	/././	/././
4.1.2	4.2.2	4.3.2	4.4.2		
4.1.3	4.2.3	4.3.3	4.4.3		
etc.	4.2.4	4.3.4	etc.		

CONSERVAT'N	ATTRIBUTION	EXHIBITION	CITATION	FACSIMILE	
3.1.1	/././	/././	3.4.1	/././	/././
3.1.2			3.4.2		
3.1.3			3.4.3		
etc.			etc.		

IDENTITY	CLASSIFIC'N	DESCRIPTION	MAKER'S MARK	INSCRIPTION	IMAGERY
2.1.1	2.2.1	2.3.1	2.4.1	2.5.1	/././
2.1.2	2.2.2	2.3.2	2.4.2	2.5.2	
2.1.3	2.2.3	2.3.3	2.4.3	2.5.3	
etc.	to 2.2.6	2.3.6	etc.	etc.	

ACQUISITION	OWNERSHIP	ASSOCIATION	ORIGIN	DERIVATION	DISCOVERY	FUNCTION
1.1.1	1.2.1	1.3.1	1.4.1		1.6.1	1.7.1
1.1.2	1.2.2	1.3.2	1.4.2		1.6.2	1.7.2
1.1.3	1.2.3	1.3.3	1.4.3		1.6.3	1.7.3
etc.	etc.	etc.	etc.		etc.	etc.

(6) TEMPLATE of data elements for <u>NATURAL SCIENCES</u> : GEOLOGY

STATUS	VALUATION	LOCATION	LOAN		
4.1.1	4.2.1	4.3.1	4.4.1	/././	/././
4.1.2	4.2.2	4.3.2	4.4.2		
4.1.3	4.2.3	4.3.3	4.4.3	/././	/././
etc.	4.2.4	4.3.4	etc.		

CONSERVAT'N	ATTRIBUTION	EXHIBITION	CITATION	FACSIMILE	
3.1.1	3.2.1		3.4.1	**	/././
3.1.2	3.2.2		3.4.2		
3.1.3	3.2.3		3.4.3		/././
etc.	etc.		etc.		

IDENTITY	CLASSIFIC'N	DESCRIPTION	MAKER'S MARK	INSCRIPTION	IMAGERY
2.1.1	2.2.1	2.3.2			
2.1.2	2.2.2	2.3.3			
2.1.3	2.2.3	2.3.4			
etc.	to 2.2.9	2.3.6			

ACQUISITION	OWNERSHIP	ASSOCIATION	ORIGIN	DERIVATION	DISCOVERY
1.1.1	1.2.1				1.6.1
1.1.2	1.2.2				1.6.2
1.1.3	1.2.3				1.6.3
etc.	etc.				etc.

** where artificial replicas (casts) of the fossil exist

APPENDIX [II]

(7) TEMPLATE of data elements for NATURAL SCIENCES : ZOOLOGY

STATUS	VALUATION	LOCATION	LOAN			
4.1.1	4.2.1	4.3.1	4.4.1	/././		/././
4.1.2	4.2.2	4.3.2	4.4.2			
4.1.3	4.2.3	4.3.3	4.4.3	/././		/././
etc.	4.2.4	4.3.4	etc.			

CONSERVAT'N	ATTRIBUTION	EXHIBITION	CITATION	FACSIMILE	
3.1.1	3.2.1		3.4.1		/././
3.1.2	3.2.2		3.4.2		
3.1.3	3.2.3		3.4.3		/././
etc.	etc.		etc.		

IDENTITY	CLASSIFIC'N	DESCRIPTION	MAKER'S MARK	INSCRIPTION	IMAGERY
2.1.1	2.2.1	2.3.2			
2.1.2	to 2.2.3	2.3.6			
2.1.3	2.2.7	2.3.7			
etc.	to 2.2.9				

ACQUISITION	OWNERSHIP	ASSOCIATION	ORIGIN	DERIVATION	DISCOVERY
1.1.1	1.2.1		** (Taxid)		1.6.1
1.1.2	1.2.2				1.6.2
1.1.3	1.2.3				1.6.3
etc.	etc.				etc.

** where details of taxidermy are to be recorded

214

Appendix III

Summary of requirements for catalogue retrieval

The following list enumerates the Elements most used for access to
records for retrieval purposes, with references to their REFORM numbers.
Selection of relevant records to be retrieved may depend on specified
attributes in these Elements used either singly or in any combination.

2.1.1	accession number
1.1.7	year of acquisition
1.1.2	method of acquisition
1.1.1	source of acquisition /loan-in
1.4.1	artist or maker
2.2.1	area of origin/ 2.2.2 country/ 2.2.3 county
2.2.4	classified by era/ 2.2.5 period/ 2.2.6 century
2.2.7	classified by object type/ 2.2.8/ 2.2.9 (3 levels)
1.3.7	named style or culture
2.3.3	material or medium
1.4.3	technique or process of production
4.3.4	current museum location
4.2.1	insurance valuation
2.1.7	previous collector's number

The above criteria are required as a general basis for all collections.
The following criteria are additional or substituted for the collections
indicated.

1.6.4	site of discovery /find-spot [Archaeology/Nat.Hist]
1.6.1	name of field collector [Archaeology/Nat.Hist]
1.7.1	function/ 1.7.2 activity/ 1.7.3 use [Social History]
2.3.7	gender of wearer and life-stage [Costume]
2.3.7	gender of animal and life-stage [Zoology]
1.4.1	issuing authority [Numismatics]
4.1.3	reason for examination /treatment [Conservation]
3.1.4	method of examination/ 3.1.5 treatment
3.1.6	materials /chemicals used in conservation
3.1.1	date of conservation treatment /inspection
3.1.2	name of conservator /external laboratory

In the absence of special indexes to other attributes, additional facility
is desirable for free-text search for retrieval of:

(i) persons' names: to retrieve references to authors,
publishers, experts (attribution), former owners and
other associated persons.

(ii) place-names: to recall localities of manufacture, sites
of topographic imagery, of exhibitions and other places
of association with the object.

Index

bowl, silver 19
boxes 10-11
broadsword 25, 98
Burckhardt, John Lewis 31
Burrell, Sir William 30
candalabrum 99, 100
cartoon 58, 61
carving 112
casting 112
Castle pattern 46-9, 114, 149
casts 149
Celynen Philharmonic 109
ceramics (Example 18) 36
ceramics (Example 25) 46
ceramics (Example 26) 50
ceremonial 116
checks 56, 59
chemical name 133
chemical reagents 144
citation 47-49
CITATION STATEMENT 148
classification 6-11, 14-5, 43, 45, 63-5
CLASSIFICATION SECTION 121
classification, by age 125-6, 147
classification, by function 116, 126
classification, by typology 122, 127-8
classification, geographic 122-5
classification, mixed 50, 122, 126
classified name; cf group name
client groups 168-9, 171
codes 73-4, 82-3, 99-101, 108, 119, 124, 183
coins 112, 120, 136
collection management 170
collector 114
common name 5, 14, 128
condition of object 155
conservation records 78-9, 93, 143-4
CONSERVATION SECTION 142
conventions 2, 6, 39, 43, 69-83, 97-9, 133
conventions, punctuation 7, 11-13, 69-71, 75, 79-81
costume 7-8, 13, 134
costume (Example 28) 63
costume (Example 29) 64
costume (Example 30) 64
costume (Example 31) 71
costume (Example 4) 20
costume classification 127
counters 56, 60
court dress 63
Cozens, J R 114
cultural environment 111

218

Hart, Gertrude   50
historical event   117
historical information   93, 105
Hobbema, Meindert   27-8, 98, 146
Hogarth, William   26, 150
holotype   155
housemark   135
ICOM   127
IDENTITY STATEMENT   118
illustrated   49, 149, 155
illustration   55-6, 60
imagery   30-1, 49, 138-9
IMAGERY STATEMENT   137
Imperial War Museum   139, 178
indexing   77-9
INSCRIPTION STATEMENT   136
inscriptions   25, 30, 33
inscriptions, cuneiform   23-4, 136
inscriptions, German   31-2, 39
insurance   157
interpretation (pictorial)   27, 137
inverted file   130, 192-3
Japanese sword   54, 72
jug   32, 129-130
keyword concept   33, 65, 72
keyword, leading   78-9, 98-9, 143
keywords, in retrieval   98, 101-2, 129
knife,fork and bodkin   31
landscape   40, 42, 138
lexicon   65-6, 79, 133, 149
life-stage   134
Linnean system   4-5, 128, 147, 155
loan report   162-3
LOAN STATEMENT   159
loans   94
loans, inward   160
loans, long-term   106
loans, outward   160-2
loans, short-term   106
local history (Example 13)   31
local history (Example 14)   32
local history (Example 5)   21-2
local history (Example 6)   23
LOCATION STATEMENT   157
maker's mark   20, 50, 112
MAKER'S MARK STATEMENT   134
maker's role   112
managerial data   152-4
managerial information   94
managerial reports   161
Marcus Aurelius   43, 150